Delta-Neutral Strategies:

A Resilient Approach to Crypto Markets

Joey Dib

Myrillion Publishings

Published by Myrillion Publishings

Printed and distributed by Amazon KDP

ISBN: 979-8-9987288-0-8

Foreword

Trading has always required adaptability in response to evolving market conditions. My professional journey began in the late 1980s during the early development of the derivatives market in France. At that time, trading floors were vibrant, characterized by manual signaling and open outcry—a stark contrast to today's rapid, data-driven trading environments. I personally experienced the industry's significant transformation with the shift towards electronic trading. This transition fundamentally reshaped market operations, enhancing accessibility while simultaneously increasing complexity and competitiveness. Interacting with leading traders globally has continually reinforced a fundamental principle: effective risk management is essential to sustainable success.

The principle of rigorous risk management is especially critical in today's cryptocurrency markets, known for extreme volatility and persistent uncertainty. Unlike traditional financial markets, supported by extensive historical data that allows a measure of predictability, crypto markets are continually evolving, making stringent risk management even more crucial. Success in trading these markets does not depend on precisely forecasting every price fluctuation; instead, it relies on structured methodologies enabling traders to adapt dynamically, safeguard their capital, and maintain consistent market engagement.

Delta-neutral strategies hold particular relevance in this challenging environment. While these methods cannot entirely remove market risks, they equip traders with robust tools to systematically manage exposure, maintain balanced positions, and significantly mitigate the impact of market volatility. This book, "Delta-Neutral Strategies: A Resilient Approach to Crypto Markets", offers a comprehensive and practical guide to mastering these techniques within real-world trading contexts. Whether your aim is to enhance your existing skill set or deepen your analytical understanding of market dynamics, the insights within these pages are intended to substantially elevate your trading proficiency.

Markets will inevitably continue their evolution, yet effective risk management remains the cornerstone of enduring success. A thorough understanding of risk management principles empowers traders to navigate uncertainties effectively and confidently seize emerging opportunities.

— Marc Despallieres, CEO of Vantage

March 2025

Table of Contents

Executive Summary

Delta-neutral strategies, once exclusive to institutional traders, are becoming more accessible in crypto markets. On-chain derivatives, DeFi lending, and algorithmic tools now enable broader participation, making these strategies scalable beyond traditional finance.

This shift marks crypto's transition from speculation to efficiency, a key sign of market maturation. As participants focus on capturing structural inefficiencies rather than price swings, crypto markets mirror the evolution of traditional financial systems.

This trend also reflects a global move toward decentralized financial coordination, shifting power from institutions to network-driven markets. The growing accessibility of delta-neutral strategies is significant both for crypto and broader financial ecosystems.

1. The Nature of Crypto Markets

Crypto markets are evolving rapidly, yet they remain inefficient compared to traditional financial markets. While traditional markets benefit from decades of refinement, regulatory oversight, and deep institutional liquidity, crypto markets are still in the early stages of maturation. This ongoing development results in persistent inefficiencies, including fragmented liquidity, price discrepancies across venues, and inconsistent funding rates—creating a fertile ground for delta-neutral strategies.

Decentralization and rapid innovation fuel continuous opportunity in crypto markets. Unlike traditional finance, where financial instruments and trading infrastructures innovation has slowed down, crypto markets constantly introduce new products, such as on-chain derivatives, algorithmic stablecoins, and AMMs. This fast-paced innovation leads to recurring inefficiencies, as new mechanisms take time to reach equilibrium and arbitrage opportunities emerge.

Currently, a convergence of favorable factors supports the application of delta-neutral strategies in crypto. Expanding institutional involvement, increasing liquidity in DeFi markets, and advancements in risk management tools make delta-neutral approaches more accessible and scalable than ever before. As the market continues to mature, participants who effectively adapt to evolving inefficiencies will remain positioned to capitalize on opportunities while minimizing exposure to volatility.

2. <u>The Nature of Delta-Neutral Strategies</u>

Delta-neutral strategies are all about precision—eliminating directional risk while taking advantage of inefficiencies in the market. Instead of betting on price movements, they focus on capturing predictable returns from pricing discrepancies, funding imbalances, and liquidity fragmentation.

Markets are far from perfect, especially in crypto, where liquidity is fragmented across venues and price disparities frequently arise. Delta-neutral strategies thrive in these inefficiencies, profiting from mispricings that need to be corrected.

Risk management is at the core of delta-neutral strategies. By maintaining a balanced exposure through hedging, diversification, and constant rebalancing, they reduce volatility and enhance capital efficiency. Instead of relying on high-risk returns, they focus on sustainable, compounding gains that allow traders to scale their strategies without increasing exposure to market shocks.

Beyond individual profits, delta-neutral strategies play a crucial role in market structure optimization. They help align prices across venues, increase liquidity depth, and stabilize funding rates, contributing to a more efficient and resilient financial ecosystem. By improving price discovery and reducing inefficiencies in both centralized and decentralized markets, these strategies reinforce stability and enhance overall market function.

3. <u>The Engine of Capital Efficiency</u>

Risk management is the foundation of all financial strategies. Without it, even profitable approaches can fail due to excessive volatility and poor capital allocation. Reducing variance is key to capital efficiency, allowing traders to optimize resource deployment and maximize returns without excessive drawdowns.

Lower variance leads to greater capital efficiency because stable returns enable more effective leverage and reinvestment. When capital is not tied up in managing large fluctuations, it can be deployed more productively, compounding gains over time.

Hedging is a primary method for reducing variance. By offsetting risks with opposing positions, hedging neutralizes exposure to adverse price movements. Whether through derivatives, or money markets, hedging ensures more consistent returns, reducing exposure to market directionality.

Delta-neutral strategies integrate hedging to achieve unmatched capital efficiency. By systematically isolating and capturing inefficiencies in crypto markets—such as funding rate disparities, price misalignments, and liquidity fragmentation—these strategies generate stable, scalable returns. The abundance of inefficiencies in crypto markets makes delta-neutral strategies particularly effective, reinforcing their role as an essential tool for maximizing risk-adjusted performance.

4. <u>Ongoing Evolution</u>

Delta-neutral strategies in crypto markets are currently benefiting from a unique confluence of factors that make them highly effective.

Expanding liquidity, increasing institutional participation, and persistent market inefficiencies create an environment where these strategies thrive. However, the landscape is not static—crypto markets evolve rapidly, requiring participants to continuously adapt to maintain their edge.

One of the most significant developments shaping this evolution is the rise of on-chain derivatives. These instruments are making hedging and structured trading more accessible, allowing delta-neutral traders to execute strategies with greater efficiency and security. Simultaneously, the integration of AI in DeFi is transforming market analysis, risk assessment, and trade execution. Just as past innovations did, these advancements are set to create new inefficiencies that agile traders can exploit before they become widely recognized.

Despite these opportunities, the fundamental challenges of crypto markets remain. Self-custody, while a core principle of DeFi, is both an advantage and a responsibility. It eliminates reliance on third parties, providing greater financial autonomy, but also places full security responsibility on the participant, increasing the risk of loss due to mismanagement or security breaches. Additionally, the unclear and shifting regulatory landscape continues to present uncertainty, with policies varying across jurisdictions and evolving in response to market developments.

As the crypto ecosystem continues to mature, delta-neutral participants must remain adaptable, leveraging new tools and strategies while carefully managing the inherent risks of self-custody and regulation. Those who can evolve alongside the market will continue to find consistent opportunities in an increasingly sophisticated trading environment.

Chapter 1: Introduction

1. Setting the Stage

Delta-neutral strategies have long been the domain of institutional players in traditional finance, reserved for those with access to advanced tools, deep market knowledge, and significant capital. These strategies, designed to profit from inefficiencies without taking directional risks, were largely inaccessible to retail investors due to high barriers to entry.

The rise of cryptocurrency markets has fundamentally transformed this landscape. Cryptocurrency markets, characterized by their unmatched volatility, rapidly evolving derivatives infrastructure, and decentralized finance (DeFi) innovations, have democratized access to delta-neutral strategies. Retail participants can now leverage these advanced strategies with minimal capital, taking full advantage of the transparency, composability, and dynamic opportunities unique to this ecosystem.

1.1) What Are Delta-Neutral Strategies?

At their core, delta-neutral strategies are designed to eliminate or minimize exposure to price movements in the underlying asset. By carefully balancing positions across various instruments, traders can isolate and profit from specific market dynamics, such as volatility, funding rates, or arbitrage opportunities. A key concept of delta-neutral strategies is to achieve high capital efficiency through the reduction of volatility. This approach enables consistent returns regardless of market direction, emphasizing market inefficiencies over speculative risks.

For example, consider a trader who holds a long position in Bitcoin but simultaneously shorts an equivalent amount through futures contracts. Any gains or losses from the Bitcoin price movement are offset by the opposing position, creating a "neutral" exposure to the asset's price. Instead, the trader's profit or loss comes from other factors, such as discrepancies between spot and futures prices.

1.2) Delta-Neutral Strategies as a Positive-Sum Activity

Delta-neutral strategies are not just another way to trade—they represent a positive-sum contribution to markets and play a key role in *market structure optimization,* the process of refining market mechanisms to promote better liquidity distribution, more accurate pricing, and efficient capital allocation. Unlike speculative trading, which often pits participants against each other in a zero-sum game, delta-neutral strategies contribute to market efficiency, enhance liquidity, and improve price discovery; reducing price distortions and inefficiencies, helping to create a more stable and functional trading environment.

In a nascent and rapidly evolving environment like cryptocurrency, the presence of delta-neutral traders serves as a stabilizing force. Rather than adding to market volatility through speculative positioning, these strategies help balance supply and demand across trading venues, ensuring that prices reflect fundamental value more accurately. This optimization is crucial for the long-term sustainability of crypto markets, attracting institutional participants and fostering a more mature financial ecosystem.

1.3) Inaccessibility in Traditional Finance

Despite their benefits, delta-neutral strategies have historically been out of reach for most retail investors in traditional finance. High barriers to entry—including restricted access to specialized derivatives markets, stringent regulatory requirements, and the necessity of advanced trading infrastructure—made these strategies the domain of well-capitalized institutional players.

Institutional firms had the resources to deploy sophisticated algorithms, leverage deep liquidity pools, and use proprietary data, all of which were critical for executing delta-neutral strategies effectively. These firms could navigate complex financial instruments with ease, benefiting from economies of scale and privileged market access, further reinforcing their dominance.

Retail participants, by contrast, faced multiple obstacles that made adoption nearly impossible. High transaction costs, limited access to derivative products, and a lack of transparent educational resources prevented individual traders from implementing these strategies. Even when retail investors could access certain markets, the inefficiencies in execution and capital limitations made them uncompetitive against institutions that operated with superior technology and liquidity advantages.

This structural disparity turned delta-neutral strategies into an exclusive tool for professional trading desks, maintaining a system where traditional financial institutions monopolized access to low-risk, delta-neutral profit opportunities. The lack of accessibility underscored the broader inefficiencies of traditional finance, where information asymmetry and institutional privilege dictated market participation.

1.4) The Era of Crypto Markets: Bridging Access and Opportunity

The emergence of cryptocurrency markets has redefined accessibility to complex financial strategies, creating a global ecosystem that operates 24/7 with unmatched transparency and innovation. Decentralized Finance (DeFi) is central to this transformation, democratizing tools like lending, borrowing, providing liquidity, and trading derivatives.

Delta-neutral strategies, once limited to well-capitalized institutions, have become accessible to retail traders through the rise of decentralized primitives and composable protocols. DeFi's interconnected structure allows participants to integrate multiple tools seamlessly, creating advanced and efficient strategies with minimal capital. This composability enables traders to achieve a level of creativity and functionality that was unattainable in traditional markets.

The unique combination of accessibility, innovation, and persistent inefficiencies in crypto markets makes them an ideal environment for delta-neutral strategies.

2. The Economic Significance of Delta-Neutral Strategies in Crypto

The emergence of cryptocurrency markets has redefined access to delta-neutral strategies, shifting from a landscape of exclusivity to one of broad participation. More than a technological breakthrough, this shift signifies an economic transition to decentralized systems and demonstrates the evolution of crypto markets from hyper-speculative trading toward structured financial mechanisms. The increasing accessibility of these strategies highlights the growing sophistication of these markets, even as they remain in a state of flux, balancing between speculative dynamics and institutional-grade financial development.

2.1) The Philosophy Behind Crypto and Financial Democratization

At its core, cryptocurrency embodies a vision of financial systems that are transparent, accessible, and resistant to centralized control. Traditional financial markets have long been dominated by institutions that act as gatekeepers, creating barriers to entry and maintaining exclusive access to sophisticated trading strategies. Crypto disrupts this model by offering open, decentralized platforms where anyone can participate in financial markets without reliance on intermediaries.

This philosophy extends beyond access—it redefines information distribution and resistance to systemic failures. Transparency, ensured by blockchain technology, allows market participants to verify transactions, reducing the need for trust in third parties. Resistance to centralized control safeguards against systemic failures that arise when financial power is concentrated in a few institutions.

The rise of delta-neutral strategies within crypto markets exemplifies this democratization. These strategies, which were once exclusive to institutional finance, are now being executed on decentralized exchanges (DEXs), permissionless lending platforms, and publicly accessible vaults. This shift represents a fundamental reordering of financial markets—one that prioritizes equal opportunity, transparency, and self-sovereign financial participation.

2.2) Shift from Speculation to Market Structure Optimization

New financial markets typically begin as hyper-speculative arenas before evolving into structured ecosystems. The early days of equities, commodities, and forex markets were driven by speculation before capital moved toward stability-enhancing mechanisms like market-making, arbitrage, and hedging. The rise of delta-neutral strategies in crypto is an indicator that the asset class is transitioning beyond its speculative phase and into an era of financial infrastructure development, though it is far from fully matured.

This transition aligns with financial market development theories, which describe how markets evolve in stages. Crypto markets have followed this pattern—starting with extreme volatility and speculative trading before moving toward sophisticated financial strategies that optimize liquidity and mitigate risk, such as the delta-neutral approach.

This illustrates that crypto markets are transitioning out of their purely speculative phase, as structured trading practices like arbitrage, market-making, and various delta-neutral strategies gain prominence. However, while these developments indicate increasing market sophistication, the crypto space continues evolving, with inefficiencies and volatility still present. This shift mirrors the early stages of financial market maturation, where hyper-speculation gradually gives way to infrastructure-building but does not fully disappear.

2.3) Shift from Centralized to Decentralized Market Structure Optimization

The rise of delta-neutral strategies also signals a shift away from centralized control toward decentralized, participant-driven financial structures. Traditional financial markets have long been dominated by intermediaries—banks, brokers, and asset managers—who extract fees for facilitating transactions, providing liquidity, and executing trades. In contrast, DeFi and decentralized trading platforms remove many of these fee-extracting intermediaries, allowing market participants to engage in trading strategies without reliance on centralized entities.

This decentralization of market structure optimization ensures that efficiency-driven strategies, such as arbitrage and liquidity provision, are no longer restricted to institutional traders. Instead, they are available to anyone with access to decentralized platforms, democratizing opportunities that a select group of financial institutions once monopolized. By leveraging smart contracts, DEXs, and permissionless financial protocols, participants can directly engage in liquidity provisioning, yield farming, and market-making activities without reliance on intermediaries.

This structural shift aligns with broader trends in technological and economic decentralization. Economist Jeremy Rifkin describes this shift as part of a global transition from centralized, hierarchical economic models to distributed, network-based systems. Just as peer-to-peer energy grids and digital networks have reshaped energy and information markets, DeFi is transforming financial coordination.

In Rifkin's vision of the Third Industrial Revolution, economic activity moves away from monopolistic intermediaries and toward decentralized, algorithm-driven infrastructures.

Delta-neutral strategies thrive in this new paradigm, where financial coordination is no longer dictated by a handful of institutions but rather by a self-organizing, low-cost system that rewards efficiency over privileged access. This transition mirrors Rifkin's concept of the Zero Marginal Cost Society, where digitization and automation drive transaction costs toward near zero, eroding traditional gatekeeping functions. In DeFi, market efficiency is no longer managed by financial institutions but by decentralized networks where liquidity, arbitrage, and market-making are driven by autonomous mechanisms rather than human intermediaries.

By making sophisticated financial tools available to all participants, the rise of delta-neutral strategies contributes to the ongoing transformation of global financial markets, aligning with broader shifts toward distributed, democratized, and cost-efficient economic systems.

2.4) The Bigger Economic Picture

The widespread adoption of delta-neutral strategies in crypto markets signals that financial markets are entering a new phase—one where efficiency, automation, and accessibility take precedence over traditional structures of privilege and intermediation. This transition is not occurring in isolation; it is part of a broader global economic shift toward decentralized coordination, algorithmic capital allocation, and the decline of intermediation-based financial structures.

Crypto markets, while still relatively small compared to traditional finance, are evolving into laboratories for financial infrastructure development. The rise of delta-neutral strategies underscores this transformation, providing a real-time indicator of how financial power is shifting toward transparency, efficiency, and direct market participation. While crypto's direct influence on the global financial system remains limited, its innovations in liquidity provision, algorithmic strategies, and decentralization are increasingly informing broader financial markets. As adoption grows, its role may become more pronounced in shaping financial infrastructure and efficiency.

3. A Unique Opportunity in Crypto Markets

Crypto markets have reached a critical juncture where maturity and inefficiency coexist to create exceptional opportunities for traders. These markets exhibit inefficiencies, high volatility, and composable decentralized structures that provide unmatched accessibility—a rare combination that makes them ideal for delta-neutral strategies.

Traders can exploit market dislocations, capitalize on rapid price movements, and seamlessly integrate DeFi tools, unlocking new avenues for innovation and profitability not available in traditional financial systems.

3.1) Market Inefficiencies: A Window of Opportunity

Despite its rapid growth, the cryptocurrency market remains relatively inefficient compared to traditional financial markets. Price dislocations, funding rate imbalances, and liquidity fragmentation across centralized exchanges and DEXs create constant opportunities for participants. Delta-neutral strategies thrive in these inefficiencies, capturing profits through various forms of arbitrage, lending, and liquidity provision.

For example, funding rates—which will be covered in depth later—display sustained inefficiencies that participants can capitalize on through basis trades to generate returns with minimal risk. As shown below, a simple basis trade with minimal leverage would yield 7%+ in 2024.

3.2) Volatility: A Catalyst for Opportunity

Volatility, traditionally seen as a measure of risk, constitutes a feature in the crypto space. Price swings of 5 to 10% in a single day are not uncommon for major cryptocurrencies, while smaller tokens can experience even greater fluctuations.

For delta-neutral strategies, this volatility is an opportunity. Strategies such as arbitrage and liquidity provision through counterparty vaults (CPVs) thrive in environments where prices are dynamic, allowing participants to capture spreads, funding rates, and premium discrepancies.

However, volatility also demands precision. Misjudging market movements or failing to maintain the neutrality of a position can lead to losses. The rapid pace of crypto markets amplifies the need for diligent monitoring and adaptive strategies.

3.3) Innovation: Derivatives and Decentralized Finance

The cryptocurrency derivatives market has experienced explosive growth in recent years. Platforms like Binance, Deribit, and Hyperliquid now provide access to perpetual swaps, options, and futures, enabling participants to hedge risks, pursue speculative opportunities, and construct complex delta-neutral strategies.

These instruments, often difficult to access for retail participants in traditional finance, have been democratized by cryptocurrency markets. Today, advanced derivatives tools are available to a much wider range of participants, creating an inclusive environment for innovation.

Similarly, DeFi protocols have experienced explosive growth since they introduced novel mechanisms for liquidity provision, lending, borrowing, and staking. These innovations have expanded the toolbox for all participants, providing unprecedented flexibility in constructing and executing strategies.

3.4) Composability: The Unique Superpower of Decentralized Finance

One of the most transformative aspects of cryptocurrency markets is the concept of composability. DeFi protocols are designed to interact seamlessly, enabling traders to stack strategies across platforms. This means users can combine lending, borrowing, liquidity provision, and hedging tools to create efficient and sophisticated strategies.

For example, a trader could stake an asset, borrow against the liquid staking token (LST), and provide liquidity to a DEX using borrowed funds. The participant is effectively combining three strategies—staking, providing liquidity, and lending as collateral for borrowing—using the same capital.

While composability allows for unparalleled capital efficiency and creativity in building advanced strategies, it is important to note that it also requires careful risk management, as it exacerbates systemic risks.

3.5) Unique Timing: Overlap Between Maturity and Inefficiency

The timing for delta-neutral strategies in cryptocurrency markets couldn't be better. Liquidity and infrastructure have matured significantly, supporting advanced strategies, while inefficiencies remain abundant enough to provide consistent opportunities. Institutional interest is surging, bringing greater stability to trading venues, yet the market is not saturated with competition. This creates a unique space for retail and semi-professional traders to thrive.

Advanced tools and platforms have also reached a new level of maturity, further enabling delta-neutral strategies. With user-friendly interfaces on exchanges and programmable DeFi smart contracts, barriers to entry have significantly decreased. Participants can now use APIs, bots, and analytics to automate strategies and respond quickly to market dynamics.

Cryptocurrency markets represent a new frontier for delta-neutral strategies, offering an unparalleled combination of volatility, market inefficiencies, composability, and accessibility through decentralized tools. This environment creates concrete opportunities for traders to exploit dislocations, hedge risks effectively, and innovate with strategies that were previously inaccessible to most.

As this book unfolds, it will provide practical insights and actionable guidance on how to harness these opportunities. The unique dynamics of cryptocurrency markets offer measurable and transformative outcomes for those equipped with the knowledge and tools to navigate them.

4. Reader Journey

This book serves as a comprehensive guide to understanding and applying delta-neutral strategies in cryptocurrency markets. It is designed to cater to readers of all levels, providing structured learning, actionable insights, and practical guidance to navigate this complex yet rewarding space.

4.1) Who Is This Book For?

- **Complete Beginners:** While market experience is irreplaceable, this book provides foundational knowledge, offering a valuable framework for understanding and navigating cryptocurrency markets.

- **Crypto-Natives:** Individuals familiar with cryptocurrency markets can deepen their knowledge of advanced financial concepts and delta-neutral strategies, exploring techniques to effectively leverage their market expertise into strategic advantage and profitability.

- **Professionals from Traditional Finance:** Experienced professionals can learn to adapt and thrive in the cryptocurrency ecosystem by leveraging the unique features of DeFi. This book highlights how to utilize DeFi's composability, transparency, and accessibility to enhance strategies and unlock new profit opportunities unavailable in traditional markets.

- **Developers and Analysts:** Developers and analysts can apply the strategies in this book to monetize their expertise, creating innovative trading tools or generating data-driven insights that uncover profitable trends.

4.2) What Will You Learn from This Book?

This book provides a structured journey through the essential principles and practical applications of delta-neutral strategies in cryptocurrency markets. Each chapter builds upon the last, equipping readers with a comprehensive understanding of market dynamics, risk management, and execution strategies.

Foundations of Financial Markets:

- Understand the fundamental roles of financial markets, including market participants, price discovery, liquidity, and efficiency.

- Explore key financial instruments, including spot markets, derivatives, fixed-income securities, and equities.

- Analyze the principles of market efficiency and inefficiencies, highlighting opportunities for delta-neutral strategies.

- Examine the structure of cryptocurrency markets and their contrast with traditional finance.

- Gain insight into centralized finance (CeFi) and DeFi, including their unique advantages and limitations.

- Learn about core DeFi components, such as DEXs, money markets, staking, tokenized yield trading, and essential trading tools.

- Understand the role of stablecoins in facilitating liquidity and risk management within crypto markets.

Foundations of Delta-Neutral Strategies:

- Learn why risk management is central to all financial market strategies, with a focus on its unique application in delta-neutral trading.

- Develop a systematic approach to identifying, measuring, and managing financial risks, including counterparty risk, market risk, and liquidity risk.

- Understand the concepts of expected value (EV) and hedging and how they apply to risk-adjusted profitability.

- Explore the principles, tools, and financial instruments used in delta-neutral strategies, including derivatives, lending markets, and structured yield opportunities.

Core Strategies:

- Master the mechanics of delta-neutral strategies, including arbitrage strategies, counterparty vaults, lending strategies, liquidity provision, staking, and yield-farming.

- Understand how incentives and tokenized yield-trading can be integrated into delta-neutral strategies to enhance portfolio performance.

- Explore practical examples and case studies that demonstrate:

- The most effective tools and platforms for executing delta-neutral strategies.

- Techniques for managing risks associated with oracles, smart contracts, and counterparty exposure.

- Common pitfalls and mistakes to avoid during real-world execution.

Current Tailwinds and Challenges:

- Explore emerging opportunities, such as the rapid expansion of on-chain derivatives and the increasing integration of AI in DeFi.

- Assess the structural inefficiencies that persist in crypto markets and how they create ongoing opportunities for delta-neutral strategies.

- Navigate current challenges in DeFi, including self-custody responsibilities and the evolving regulatory landscape.

The Bigger Picture:

- Synthesize everything learned in this book to construct a holistic understanding of delta-neutral strategies and develop a nuanced perspective on why delta-neutral strategies exist, how they enhance market efficiency, and their practical implementation in both centralized and decentralized financial ecosystems.

4.3) What Does This Book Aim to Accomplish?

This book provides a structured and comprehensive approach to delta-neutral strategies in cryptocurrency markets. By combining foundational knowledge with practical execution, it equips traders with the tools needed to navigate and capitalize on market inefficiencies effectively.

Key Outcomes Include:

- **Building a Strong Foundation:** Establishing a deep understanding of financial principles essential for successfully applying delta-neutral strategies in cryptocurrency markets.

- **Navigating the Cryptocurrency Ecosystem:** Understanding the defining features of cryptocurrency markets, their inefficiencies, and how CeFi and DeFi frameworks shape trading opportunities.

- **Developing Risk Management Skills:** Learning how to identify, measure, and mitigate risks, ensuring sustainable and effective trading practices.

- **Implementing Core Strategies:** Mastering key delta-neutral strategies such as arbitrage, counterparty vaults, lending loops, and liquidity provision, alongside the practical tools necessary for real-world execution.

- **Adapting to Challenges and Opportunities:** Addressing evolving market conditions, including regulatory risks, custodial challenges, and emerging innovations such as on-chain derivatives and AI-driven optimization.

By the end of this book, readers will be able to construct, execute, and refine delta-neutral strategies with precision. Whether developing a foundational understanding or enhancing advanced techniques, this content is structured to provide actionable insights at every level. By focusing on execution and emerging trends, this book ensures that traders are prepared to seize opportunities while mitigating risks in an evolving financial landscape.

Chapter 2: Foundations of Financial Markets

Financial markets enable asset exchange, price discovery, and capital allocation, forming the basis of global finance. Understanding these markets is essential for navigating both traditional and cryptocurrency trading environments.

This chapter is divided into two parts: the first focuses on traditional financial markets, covering key instruments, market participants, and principles of market efficiency and inefficiency. The second explores cryptocurrency markets, contrasting them with traditional finance and examining the innovations and challenges unique to DeFi. Mastering these concepts is crucial for executing delta-neutral strategies effectively.

1. **Market Fundamentals**

Understanding market fundamentals is essential for traders to navigate financial systems effectively. This section explores the foundational principles of financial markets, the roles of key participants, price formation mechanisms, market efficiency, and inefficiencies that create trading opportunities.

1.1) What Are Markets and Their Core Functions?

Financial markets serve as the foundation of economic activity, enabling the exchange of assets, efficient price discovery, and the allocation of capital. These markets facilitate transactions between buyers and sellers, ensuring liquidity and stability in financial ecosystems.

Core Functions of Markets

- **Price Discovery:** Markets aggregate supply and demand, allowing asset prices to reflect collective participant sentiment and information.

- **Liquidity Provision:** By offering a venue for continuous trading, markets ensure that assets can be bought or sold efficiently without significant price disruption.

- **Capital Allocation:** Markets direct capital toward productive uses by enabling businesses, governments, and individuals to raise funds for investments.

- **Risk Transfer:** Through derivatives and hedging mechanisms, markets allow participants to manage financial risks, reducing exposure to adverse price movements.

Types of Financial Markets

- **Equities:** Stock markets enable the trading of company shares, reflecting ownership stakes and corporate performance.

- **Fixed Income:** Bond markets facilitate lending and borrowing through debt securities issued by governments and corporations.

- **Foreign Exchange (Forex):** Forex markets allow for the exchange of global currencies, impacting trade and economic stability.

- **Commodities:** Markets for physical goods such as oil, gold, and agricultural products provide pricing transparency and risk management for producers and consumers.

- **Cryptocurrency Markets:** Digital asset markets operate within decentralized and centralized platforms, introducing new dynamics of liquidity, volatility, and transparency.

Takeaway

Financial markets exist to facilitate trade, ensure liquidity, and allocate capital efficiently. They provide a structured environment where buyers and sellers interact to determine asset prices based on supply and demand. Different types of markets, from equities to commodities and forex, serve distinct roles but share common principles of price discovery, liquidity, and risk transfer. Recognizing these functions helps traders and investors better navigate market dynamics and optimize their strategies.

1.2) Key Market Participants and Their Roles

Understanding the key participants in financial markets is essential for analyzing market behavior, liquidity dynamics, and price movements. Each participant plays a distinct role in shaping market efficiency, volatility, and overall stability.

Types of Market Participants in Traditional Finance

- **Exchanges and Brokers:** Facilitate market transactions by connecting buyers and sellers, ensuring fair trade execution, and providing essential infrastructure for trading activity.

- **Market Makers:** Maintain liquidity by continuously quoting buy and sell prices, narrowing bid-ask spreads, and reducing price volatility.

- **Institutional Investors:** Hedge funds, mutual funds, pension funds, and insurance companies that deploy significant capital, influencing price trends and market stability.

- **Proprietary Trading Firms:** Trade using their own capital to capitalize on market inefficiencies, often utilizing high-frequency trading (HFT) and algorithmic strategies.

- **Banks and Financial Institutions:** Provide credit, facilitate capital markets, underwrite securities, and engage in large-scale transactions that impact liquidity.

- **Retail Investors:** Individual traders and investors participating in markets for wealth growth, speculation, or hedging, contributing to market sentiment and liquidity.

- **Regulators and Policymakers:** Organizations such as the SEC, CFTC, and central banks that establish and enforce rules, ensuring transparency, stability, and investor protection.

Market Participants' Influence on Efficiency and Volatility

- **Price Formation and Order Flow:** Institutions and proprietary trading firms influence price discovery by placing large orders that shape liquidity. Market makers continuously adjust bid-ask spreads to reflect changing supply and demand, while retail investors add order flow diversity and momentum.

- **Liquidity and Market Stability:** Institutional investors provide deep liquidity, which stabilizes price movements, while speculative trading by retail participants can create short-term volatility. Market makers and banks can act as stabilizing forces by supplying liquidity during market downturns.

- **Arbitrage Strategies:** Arbitrage strategies exploit inefficiencies, capturing price discrepancies across different exchanges and instruments. HFT firms leverage speed and data analysis to profit from minute price movements, enhancing market efficiency but sometimes exacerbating volatility during market stress.

Takeaways

Financial markets consist of various participants, each with a specific role in ensuring liquidity, stability, and efficiency. Exchanges and brokers connect buyers and sellers, while market makers and institutional investors drive liquidity and price trends. Proprietary trading firms capitalize on inefficiencies, banks provide critical financial infrastructure, and retail investors contribute to market sentiment and momentum. Regulators oversee market integrity, ensuring fair and transparent operations. Understanding these roles allows traders to anticipate market movements and refine their strategies accordingly.

1.3) Market Dynamics and Price Formation

Market dynamics refer to the forces that drive price movements and liquidity conditions in financial markets. These forces shape how assets are valued and traded, influenced by interactions between market participants, macroeconomic factors, and structural market conditions. Understanding these dynamics is essential for assessing market behavior and developing informed trading strategies.

Key Characteristics of Markets

- **Liquidity:** The ability to buy or sell assets without significantly impacting their price. These markets display lower bid-ask spreads and lower slippage.

- **Volatility:** The degree of price fluctuation over time. Highly volatile markets present both risks and opportunities for traders.

- **Transparency:** The extent to which market information, such as trading volume and price data, is available to participants.

- **Efficiency:** The speed and accuracy with which market prices reflect all available information. Efficient markets reduce arbitrage opportunities, while inefficiencies create exploitable trading conditions.

Key Drivers of Market Dynamics

- **Supply and Demand Forces:** Prices fluctuate based on the balance between buying and selling pressure. When demand exceeds supply, prices rise; when supply surpasses demand, prices decline.

- **Liquidity:** The depth of market orders influences price stability and execution efficiency. High liquidity results in smoother price movements, while low liquidity can lead to sharp price swings.

- **Macroeconomic and External Factors:** Interest rates, inflation, central bank policies, and geopolitical events play significant roles in shaping market conditions and investor sentiment.

These key drivers interact continuously, shaping the overall market environment. Supply and demand fluctuations determine price trends, while liquidity conditions affect how smoothly trades can be executed. Macroeconomic events, such as central bank rate decisions or geopolitical instability, can cause sudden shifts in investor sentiment, leading to volatility. Understanding these elements allows traders to anticipate price movements and assess risk levels effectively, ensuring a more strategic approach to trading and investment decisions.

Price Formation Mechanisms

- **Order Books and Trade Execution:** Market prices are set by the continuous interaction of buy and sell orders. The highest bid and lowest ask determine the spread, affecting transaction costs. A narrow spread typically indicates a more liquid and efficient market, reflecting strong trading activity and minimal price discrepancies.

- **Price Discovery in Different Markets:** In the liquid market, transparent order books facilitate price formation, while private or over-the-counter (OTC) markets rely on negotiated pricing, which can introduce pricing inefficiencies.

- **Market Microstructure:** Factors such as bid-ask spreads, order flow, and slippage impact the efficiency and cost of executing trades.

Together, these mechanisms define how prices are established and adjusted in financial markets. Order books play a crucial role in real-time price setting, ensuring that buy and sell orders interact efficiently. In liquid markets, price discovery is swift, reflecting available information and trader sentiment. In contrast, markets with wider spreads, lower transparency, or reduced liquidity can lead to inefficiencies that create more arbitrage opportunities. Traders who understand these dynamics can better navigate different market environments, optimize execution, and capitalize on mispricings.

Takeaways

Market dynamics shape the behavior of financial markets by determining how prices move and liquidity is distributed. The mechanisms of price formation, such as order books and market microstructure, dictate how efficiently markets process information. Recognizing these factors helps traders anticipate price movements, manage risks, and refine their trading strategies for better execution and profitability.

1.4) Market Efficiency and Its Implications

Market efficiency is a widely studied concept in financial markets, describing the extent to which asset prices reflect available information. According to traditional economic theory, an efficient market should prevent participants from consistently achieving excess returns without taking additional risks. However, the degree to which markets truly function efficiently remains a topic of debate. Understanding market efficiency is crucial for traders and investors as it shapes the effectiveness of different trading strategies and determines the potential for exploiting price anomalies.

The Efficient Market Hypothesis

The Efficient Market Hypothesis (EMH) is a theoretical framework that classifies market efficiency into three forms:

- **Weak Form Efficiency:** Prices reflect all past trading information, such as historical prices and volume. This suggests that technical analysis, which relies on historical price patterns, cannot consistently generate excess returns.

- **Semi-Strong Form Efficiency:** Prices incorporate all publicly available information, including financial statements, news releases, and economic data. In such markets, fundamental analysis may have limited effectiveness.

- **Strong Form Efficiency:** Prices reflect all information, both public and private (insider knowledge). In a perfectly efficient market, even insider trading would not yield excess profits.

While the EMH provides a structured way to evaluate efficiency, real-world markets often exhibit varying degrees of inefficiency, influenced by liquidity constraints, behavioral biases, and market structure.

How Information Is Incorporated Into Prices

- **News and Economic Data:** Market prices adjust to new information, such as central bank decisions, corporate earnings, and geopolitical developments, though the speed and accuracy of this adjustment may vary.

- **High-Frequency and Algorithmic Trading:** Sophisticated trading algorithms contribute to efficiency by rapidly processing and responding to information, narrowing bid-ask spreads, and reducing pricing errors.

- **Investor Sentiment and Reaction Times:** Behavioral biases, such as overreaction or underreaction to news, can temporarily disrupt efficiency and create short-lived opportunities for informed traders.

While efficient markets should, in theory, reflect new information instantly, in practice, inefficiencies can persist due to delays in information dissemination, irrational investor behavior, and structural constraints in financial systems. These inefficiencies create opportunities for traders who can identify mispricings and act swiftly.

Takeaway

Market efficiency is not absolute, and its degree varies across financial markets. While efficient markets quickly incorporate new information, inefficiencies can persist due to behavioral biases, liquidity constraints, and structural barriers. These inefficiencies create opportunities for traders who can recognize mispricings and act accordingly. Understanding the limitations of the EMH helps traders refine their strategies and identify market conditions where inefficiencies can be exploited for consistent returns.

1.5) Market Inefficiencies and Trading Opportunities

Despite the assumptions of the EMH, financial markets often exhibit inefficiencies that create opportunities for traders to achieve excess returns. These inefficiencies arise due to structural limitations, behavioral biases, liquidity constraints, and asymmetrical access to information. Identifying and exploiting these inefficiencies is key to developing profitable trading strategies.

Types of Market Inefficiencies

- **Pricing Inefficiencies:** Occur when asset prices deviate from their fundamental or fair value, leading to mispricing. These inefficiencies can also come in the form of arbitrage opportunities, where the same asset trades at different prices across markets.

- **Rate Inefficiencies:** Arise when funding, lending, or borrowing rates do not accurately reflect market conditions. In perpetual futures markets, funding rates can become disconnected from the true cost of holding a position, leading to exploitable distortions. Similarly, lending and borrowing rates may vary significantly across DeFi and CeFi platforms, even for similar assets and risk profiles. Yield curve inefficiencies can also emerge, where short-term and long-term rates exhibit anomalies, such as inverted yield curves in DeFi.

- **Volatility Inefficiencies:** Occur when market participants misprice or mismanage volatility risk. A common example is the mismatch between implied volatility (as priced into options) and realized volatility (actual market fluctuations). Additionally, volatility risk premiums may be inconsistent across assets, leading to mispriced hedging instruments.

These inefficiencies highlight the imperfections in financial markets, demonstrating that price movements are not always purely rational or immediate. Recognizing these inefficiencies allows traders to develop strategies that capitalize on predictable mispricings, reinforcing the importance of a structured and informed approach to trading.

Causes for Market Inefficiency

- **Informational Causes:** Arise when markets fail to process information efficiently. Asymmetric information gives some traders an advantage, while slow information diffusion delays price adjustments. Misinterpretation of data leads to pricing errors, and manipulation tactics like wash trading and spoofing distort price discovery.

- **Structural Causes:** Stem from market design and regulation. Market fragmentation spreads liquidity across platforms, creating price discrepancies. Latency arbitrage exploits execution delays, while regulatory barriers and capital constraints prevent efficient arbitrage. Other factors such as tick size constraints and order-book rigidities further contribute to inefficiencies.

- **Liquidity-Driven Causes:** Occur when market depth is insufficient for smooth price formation. Order-book imbalances and forced liquidations create short-term mispricings. Inefficient market-making leads to wide spreads and slippage, while low-liquidity assets experience significant price impact.

- **Behavioral Causes:** Result from irrational decision-making. Herding behavior amplifies inefficiencies, while overreaction or underreaction to news distorts prices. Cognitive biases like confirmation bias and loss aversion lead to suboptimal trading, and speculative frenzies driven by FOMO inflate asset prices beyond fundamentals.

Exploiting Market Inefficiencies

- **Price and Volatility Based Strategies:** Take advantage of price and implied volatility inefficiencies across markets.
    - Spatial arbitrage buys an asset on one exchange and sells it on another where the price is higher.
    - Triangular arbitrage uses three currency pairs within the same exchange to exploit pricing mismatches.
    - Index arbitrage trades differences between an index's value and its underlying assets.
    - Implied volatility arbitrage profits from discrepancies in implied volatility between multiple instruments.
- **Rate and Yield Based Strategies:** Take advantage of rate and yield inefficiencies across markets.
    - Cash-and-carry arbitrage exploits the difference between spot and futures prices by buying in the spot market and shorting futures.
    - Funding rate arbitrage profits from varying funding rates in perpetual futures across different exchanges.
    - Yield farming optimization moves funds between DeFi protocols to maximize performance.
    - Interest rate arbitrage borrows where interest rates are low and lends where they are high.

Takeaway

Financial markets are not always perfectly efficient, which means that price discrepancies, liquidity gaps, and irrational behaviors create opportunities for traders. Understanding how and why inefficiencies occur is essential for identifying profitable trading opportunities and mitigating risk. Participants who are aware of and recognize these inefficiencies can capitalize on them through arbitrage, statistical, liquidity provision, and rate exploitation strategies. This book will focus on some of these activities, which are core to delta-neutral strategies.

2. Key Financial Instruments in Traditional Markets

Traditional financial markets offer a broad range of instruments that serve various economic functions, from capital formation to risk management. These instruments form the backbone of modern finance, allowing investors, institutions, and governments to allocate capital efficiently, hedge exposure, and speculate on price movements. This section explores the core financial instruments—spot markets, fixed-income securities, and derivatives—and their roles within the financial system. It also examines how different markets interact, influencing liquidity, volatility, and systemic risk. Understanding these instruments is essential for drawing parallels with crypto markets and identifying how financial strategies evolve in decentralized ecosystems.

2.1) Spot Markets

A spot market is a financial market where assets are bought and sold for immediate delivery. In contrast to derivatives markets, which involve contracts that settle in the future, spot transactions are settled on the spot or within a short period. This immediacy makes spot markets foundational to financial systems, providing a transparent mechanism for price discovery and liquidity.

Spot markets exist across various asset classes, including equities, commodities, forex, and cryptocurrencies. Unlike fixed-income instruments, which provide scheduled returns, spot market valuations are entirely market-driven and fluctuate based on supply and demand dynamics.

Examples of Spot Markets

Spot markets cover a wide range of assets, each serving different functions in financial markets:

- **Equities (Stocks):** Shares of publicly traded companies trade in spot markets such as the New York Stock Exchange (NYSE) and NASDAQ. Investors buy and sell stocks for immediate ownership, with prices determined by market supply and demand.

- **Foreign Exchange (Forex):** The forex spot market allows traders to exchange one currency for another at prevailing exchange rates. It is the largest and most liquid financial market globally.

- **Commodities:** Physical commodities like gold, oil, and agricultural products are traded on spot markets where buyers receive immediate delivery of the asset.

- **Cryptocurrencies:** Digital assets such as Bitcoin and Ethereum trade on spot exchanges, where users buy and sell tokens at real-time market prices.

Speculation

Spot markets are widely used for speculative trading, where participants buy assets expecting price appreciation. This approach is common in equity markets, commodities, and cryptocurrencies, where traders aim to profit from upward price movements.

Unlike derivatives, spot markets do not offer built-in leverage, requiring traders to commit full capital upfront. While this limits potential returns, it also reduces liquidation risk compared to leveraged positions.

Hedging (Limited Role)

While spot markets are not the most efficient tool for hedging because of the lack of leverage, they can be used to balance exposure within a portfolio.

For example, a commodity producer may hold a certain quantity of raw materials in the spot market to hedge against supply chain disruptions.

Arbitrage

Spot markets provide a basis for arbitrage strategies, where traders exploit price discrepancies across different platforms or instruments.

- **Cross-Exchange Arbitrage:** Traders purchase an asset on one exchange where it is priced lower and sell it on another exchange where the price is higher. For example, ETH trades at $1,900 on Exchange A and $1,920 on Exchange B. A trader buys ETH on Exchange A and simultaneously sells it on Exchange B to capture the $20 spread.

- **Basis Trading:** Traders capitalize on price differences between the spot market and futures contracts. For example, a trader buys Bitcoin in the spot market while simultaneously selling Bitcoin futures at a premium. When the futures contract approaches expiry, the trader closes both positions, capturing the price difference as profit.

Takeaways

Spot markets are where assets are bought and sold for immediate settlement, making them essential for price discovery and liquidity. They are best suited for speculation and arbitrage but are less effective for hedging compared to derivatives. While they lack leverage, they offer lower risk and greater transparency, making them foundational to financial markets.

2.2) Fixed-Income Instruments

Fixed-income instruments are debt securities that provide periodic interest payments and return the principal at maturity. They offer predictable cash flows, making them essential for capital preservation and income generation. Unlike equities, which provide ownership in a company and variable returns, fixed-income instruments are contractual obligations that prioritize stability over growth potential.

These securities serve a crucial role in financial markets, influencing monetary policy, corporate financing, and investment strategies. Investors use fixed-income instruments for income generation, risk management, and macroeconomic positioning.

Government Bonds (Treasuries, Sovereign Debt)

Government bonds are issued by national governments to finance public expenditures. They are considered low-risk investments due to the backing of sovereign entities.

- **Hedging:** Investors use government bonds to mitigate risk during economic downturns.

- **Income Generation:** Treasuries provide reliable interest payments, making them attractive for conservative portfolios.

- **Macroeconomic Positioning:** Bond yields reflect central bank policies and economic expectations.

Corporate Bonds (Investment-Grade vs. High-Yield)

Corporate bonds are issued by companies to raise capital, with risk levels categorized as investment-grade or high-yield. Investment-grade bonds, issued by financially stable companies, offer lower yields with minimal default risk. High-yield bonds, or junk bonds, come with higher credit risk but offer greater returns. Investors select these based on their risk appetite and income goals.

- **Income Generation:** Corporate bonds often offer higher yields than government securities, compensating for increased risk.

- **Risk Diversification:** Investors balance portfolios by mixing corporate and government debt.

- **Speculation:** Traders buy and sell corporate bonds based on financial outlooks and credit conditions.

Municipal Bonds (Tax-Exempt Investments)

Municipal bonds are issued by local governments and municipalities to fund infrastructure projects, such as schools and highways.

- **Tax Efficiency:** Many municipal bonds offer tax-exempt interest income, benefiting high-net-worth individuals.

- **Local Government Financing:** Municipalities rely on bond issuances to fund public services and development projects.

Structured Fixed-Income Products (Mortgage-Backed Securities, Collateralized Debt Obligations)

Structured fixed-income products bundle debt instruments, such as mortgages and loans, into securities that offer varying levels of risk and return. These products use tranching mechanisms to allocate different levels of credit risk, allowing investors to choose exposure suited to their risk tolerance.

- **Yield Enhancement:** Structured debt provides opportunities for higher returns than traditional fixed income.

- **Credit Risk Management:** Investors choose securities with different risk exposures based on tranche structure.

Interconnections with the Broader Market

Fixed-income markets are closely linked to equities and broader macroeconomic conditions. Rising interest rates typically lower stock valuations by increasing borrowing costs and discount rate on future cash flows, prompting investors to shift between bonds and equities depending on risk appetite and yield expectations.

Additionally, bond market movements serve as economic indicators; yield curve inversions have historically predicted recessions, while bond yields influence central bank policies and investor sentiment. Since bond prices and yields move inversely, rising interest rates generally lead to bond price declines, impacting fixed-income portfolios. Central bank policies play a crucial role in setting interest rate expectations and shaping investor sentiment in fixed-income markets.

Takeaways

Fixed-income instruments provide a predictable income stream and are widely used for capital preservation and risk management. Government bonds offer lower returns but greater security, while corporate and structured debt instruments provide higher yields with increased risk. Interest rates play a central role in fixed-income markets, impacting bond prices and investor sentiment. Understanding these dynamics helps investors make informed decisions about income generation, risk diversification, and macroeconomic positioning.

2.3) Derivatives

Derivatives are financial instruments whose value is derived from an underlying asset, such as stocks, commodities, bonds, or cryptocurrencies. Unlike spot markets, where assets are traded for immediate delivery, derivatives allow traders to gain exposure to an asset without directly owning it.

Derivatives can be standardized and traded on regulated exchanges (e.g., futures and options) or customized through over-the-counter (OTC) agreements (e.g., forwards and swaps). These instruments play a crucial role in risk management, speculation, and market efficiency.

Futures and Forwards

Futures and forwards are agreements to buy or sell an asset at a predetermined price on a future date. The difference between the two is that futures contracts are standardized and traded on exchanges, providing transparency and reducing counterparty risk through clearinghouses, while forwards are customized agreements traded OTC, offering flexibility but carrying higher counterparty risk.

- **Hedging:** Businesses lock in prices to manage risk (e.g., a wheat farmer selling futures contracts to secure a stable selling price for their crops).

- **Speculation:** Traders use leverage to bet on price movements, amplifying both gains and losses.

- **Arbitrage:** Market participants exploit price differences between futures and spot markets.

Futures and forwards serve as essential tools for managing risk and capitalizing on market movements. They play a critical role in financial markets, offering liquidity, hedging opportunities, and speculative potential.

Options

Options are contracts that grant the holder the right, but not the obligation, to buy (call option) or sell (put option) an asset at a specified price before or on a predetermined expiration date. This flexibility makes options valuable for hedging, speculation, and volatility trading.

- **Hedging:** Investors use options to protect portfolios from adverse price movements (e.g., buying put options to guard against stock declines).

- **Speculation:** Options enable leveraged directional bets with predefined risks, allowing traders to gain exposure to asset price movements without needing full capital upfront.

- **Volatility Trading:** Options allow traders to take positions based on expected volatility changes, profiting from discrepancies between implied and realized volatility.

Compared to futures, options offer more strategic flexibility, as they provide asymmetric risk-reward structures. While futures obligate both parties to execute the contract, options grant the choice to exercise, which can be beneficial in uncertain markets. This makes them a preferred instrument for traders looking to hedge downside risk while maintaining upside potential.

Swaps

Swaps are financial contracts in which two parties agree to exchange cash flows or financial instruments based on predefined conditions. Unlike futures and options, swaps are typically traded OTC, allowing for customization but introducing counterparty risk. Common types include interest rate swaps, currency swaps, and credit default swaps (CDS).

- **Hedging:** Companies use swaps to manage interest rates and currency risks. For example, a firm with a floating-rate loan may enter a swap to exchange it for a fixed-rate loan, reducing exposure to interest rate fluctuations.

- **Yield Enhancement:** Financial institutions or investors looking to increase returns may act as the counterparty to firms seeking to hedge interest rate risk. For example, a lender holding fixed-rate assets might enter into a swap agreement to exchange fixed-rate returns for floating-rate returns, capitalizing on potential interest rate increases while providing the counterparty with a predictable cost structure.

Swaps play a crucial role in financial markets by allowing institutions to customize risk management strategies that would be difficult to achieve through standard exchange-traded instruments. However, since swaps are not traded on centralized exchanges (CEXs), creditworthiness and contract enforcement are key considerations for participants.

Interplay with Spot Markets

Derivatives markets and spot markets are deeply interconnected, with price movements in one often impacting the other. Futures and options serve as tools for managing exposure and speculating on future price trends, while also contributing to price discovery.

Basis trading is the primary mechanism that ensures derivatives prices stay aligned with the underlying asset's spot price. Traders engaging in basis trading capitalize on the spread between spot and futures prices, which naturally converges as contracts approach expiration, allowing them to secure near-zero risk returns.

Additionally, imbalances in derivatives markets, such as excessive speculation or sudden unwinding of positions, can create ripple effects in spot markets. Understanding these interactions helps traders refine their strategies, whether they seek to hedge risk or capitalize on market fluctuations.

Takeaways

Derivatives allow traders to manage risk, speculate, and find arbitrage opportunities without directly owning assets. Futures and forwards help lock in prices, options offer flexibility in market participation, and swaps allow customization of financial exposure. While derivatives enhance financial strategies, they introduce leverage and counterparty risks. The close relationship between derivatives and spot markets ensures price alignment, with basis trading playing a key role in this equilibrium. Understanding these instruments allows market participants to optimize their trading and risk management approaches.

2.4) Interconnections Across Markets

Financial markets do not operate in isolation; they are deeply interconnected through capital flows, risk transfers, and macroeconomic influences. Changes in one market often trigger reactions in others, creating opportunities and risks for traders and investors. Similar concepts of interconnection apply to cryptocurrency markets, where, for example, lending rates, funding rates, and staking yields influence each other. This will be explored in more detail later in the book. Understanding these relationships is crucial for managing risk, identifying arbitrage opportunities, and anticipating price movements across asset classes.

Spot vs. Derivatives Markets

Derivatives prices are directly linked to the underlying assets in spot markets. Futures and options derive their value from spot prices, while derivatives also provide feedback by influencing price discovery in spot markets. Arbitrage strategies ensure that significant price discrepancies between spot and derivative markets are corrected over time.

The continuous interaction through basis trading keeps derivatives prices aligned with spot prices. This is because traders are increasingly incentivized to exploit price discrepancies between the two markets as they grow to generate near-zero risk returns. This ensures that market forces correct mispricings as contracts approach expiration, thereby maintaining market efficiency.

Fixed Income vs. Equities

Fixed-income and equity markets are closely linked through interest rates. Bond yields serve as a benchmark for discounting future cash flows, affecting stock valuations. When bond yields rise, equities often decline due to higher discount rates, making future earnings less attractive. For example, when the Federal Reserve raises interest rates, high-growth stocks, which rely on future earnings, typically decline as their valuations are more sensitive to discount rate changes.

Rising interest rates increase the attractiveness of fixed-income investments relative to equities by offering higher yields with lower risk. This dynamic also tends to lead to capital outflows from equities into bonds, particularly during periods of economic tightening, as investors seek safer, income-generating assets.

Higher rates also raise corporate borrowing costs, pressuring equity valuations by reducing expected future earnings.

Derivatives vs. Fixed-Income Markets

Interest rate derivatives, such as swaps and futures, are closely tied to fixed-income markets. Interest rate swaps play a crucial role in shaping fixed-income markets by influencing yield curves, market liquidity, and risk transfer mechanisms.

Swap rates serve as benchmarks for fixed-income pricing, affecting government and corporate bond yields. Institutions use these instruments to hedge interest rate fluctuations, which in turn impacts bond demand and pricing.

CDS serve as market-based indicators of credit risk, influencing corporate bond pricing by reflecting market sentiment on the likelihood of default. A widening CDS spread suggests growing concerns about a borrower's creditworthiness, which can lead to higher borrowing costs and declining bond prices.

Macroeconomic Events and Market Reactions

Macroeconomic factors, such as inflation, GDP growth, and central bank policies, create ripple effects across multiple asset classes. Traders and investors closely monitor these developments to adjust their portfolios.

Central Bank Policy:

- Interest rate hikes strengthen bonds but often pressure equities and risk assets.

- Liquidity injections boost investor appetite for equities and riskier assets.

Economic Indicators:

- Strong GDP growth generally supports equities but can lead to higher interest rates.

- Inflation surprises impact bonds, equities, and derivatives, leading to cross-asset volatility.

Takeaways

Financial markets are deeply interconnected, with movements in one asset class influencing others. Interest rates serve as a key driver, shaping capital flows between fixed income, equities, and derivatives. Basis trading plays a critical role in aligning derivatives prices with spot markets, preventing mispricing and ensuring efficiency. Understanding these relationships helps traders and investors anticipate trends, manage risk effectively, and capitalize on arbitrage opportunities in an evolving financial landscape.

2.5) Case Study: Market Event Analysis

A market event is a significant occurrence that disrupts or influences financial markets, often triggering widespread volatility and capital reallocation. These events can stem from economic policy shifts, regulatory changes, financial crises, or geopolitical developments. This subsection will analyze the 2022 Federal Reserve rate hikes to provide a practical understanding of how different asset classes react to such disruptions, helping traders and investors anticipate risk, hedge exposure, and seize opportunities across markets.

Event Overview: The Cross-Market Impact of 2022 Federal Reserve Rate Hikes

In 2022, the Federal Reserve launched its most aggressive rate hiking cycle in decades to combat inflation, which peaked at 9.1% in June. Inflation was fueled by pandemic-driven stimulus, supply chain disruptions, and the Russia-Ukraine war, which spiked energy and food prices. In response, the Fed raised rates seven times, starting with 25 basis points in March and escalating to four consecutive 75 basis point hikes before slowing to 50 basis points in December, ending the year at 4.25–4.50%.

This shift in monetary policy led to a broad market repricing, affecting fixed income, equities, derivatives, and currency markets:

- **Fixed Income:** Treasury yields surged as bond prices fell, with short-duration bonds declining less than long-duration bonds due to their lower sensitivity to rate changes.

- **Equities:** Growth stocks, particularly in the technology sector, experienced sharp declines as higher discount rates reduced their future earnings valuations, while value stocks and defensive sectors outperformed.

- **Derivatives:** Volatility increased across futures and options markets as traders adjusted their hedging strategies and speculators sought to capitalize on rate-driven movements.

- **Spot Forex Markets:** The US dollar strengthened significantly as higher yields attracted capital inflows, leading to declines in risk-sensitive currencies.

These reactions highlight the interconnected nature of financial markets. The Fed's rate hikes drove investors away from riskier assets like growth stocks and long-duration bonds, leading to capital shifts into defensive equities and short-duration bonds. Higher bond yields made equities less attractive, prompting sector rotations and increasing demand for derivative hedging strategies. Meanwhile, the strengthened US dollar created ripple effects across global forex markets, making US assets more appealing to international investors but pressuring emerging market currencies.

Lessons Learned

- Interest rate policy is a major driver of cross-asset price movements. The repricing of bonds directly impacts equity valuations, forex markets, and derivative hedging strategies.

- Market interconnections create both risks and opportunities. Understanding how different asset classes react enables more effective hedging and speculative positioning.

- Risk management is crucial in volatile environments. The ability to adjust exposure across asset classes helps mitigate portfolio drawdowns and maximize returns.

3.   Bridging Traditional and Crypto Markets

The transition from traditional financial markets to cryptocurrency markets introduces fundamental differences in market structure, trading mechanisms, and financial products. Unlike traditional finance, where institutions, central banks, and regulatory frameworks dictate market rules, crypto markets operate within a blend of CeFi and DeFi.

This section explores how crypto markets differ from traditional markets, their unique inefficiencies and opportunities, the dominance of perpetual futures, and the interplay between CeFi and DeFi in shaping the crypto financial ecosystem.

3.1) Contrasts with Traditional Markets

Cryptocurrency markets differ significantly from traditional financial markets in their structure, efficiency, and regulatory landscape. While crypto introduces innovative financial mechanisms, it remains a young and evolving market with inefficiencies that create both risks and opportunities. Unlike traditional finance, which operates under strict regulation with well-defined settlement and risk management systems, crypto markets function across a blend of CeFi platforms and DeFi protocols. This combination influences trading hours, liquidity distribution, and overall market behavior, contributing to volatility and arbitrage opportunities.

Crypto Market Maturity and Inefficiencies

While crypto markets are in the process of maturing, they remain inefficient compared to traditional financial markets. Many inefficiencies are similar to those seen in the early days of traditional finance, presenting both risks and opportunities.

- **Liquidity Fragmentation:** Trading is spread across CeFi exchanges, DeFi platforms, and OTC markets, leading to inconsistent liquidity depth and price discrepancies.

- **Regulatory Uncertainty:** Lack of clear regulations creates hesitation among institutional players, limiting market efficiency.

- **Market Structure Gaps:** Crypto markets lack central clearing, leading to arbitrage opportunities such as cross-exchange price differences and funding rate mispricings.

- **High Volatility:** Crypto remains heavily retail-driven, leading to exaggerated price swings, speculative bubbles, and liquidation cascades.

Market Structure and Trading Hours

Traditional financial markets operate within fixed trading hours, with exchanges like the NYSE and NASDAQ following a set schedule. In contrast, cryptocurrency markets are open 24/7, allowing for continuous trading across global CEXs and DEXs. This always-on nature leads to constant liquidity flows but also contributes to higher volatility and price inefficiencies compared to traditional markets.

Settlement and Custody

In traditional finance, trades typically settle within two business days (T+2), requiring intermediaries, such as clearinghouses and custodians, to ensure smooth transactions. Crypto markets, on the other hand, offer near-instant settlement via blockchain networks. While instant settlement increases efficiency, it also introduces new risks, including security vulnerabilities and counterparty risks in CeFi.

Market Participants and Liquidity Providers

Traditional finance is dominated by institutional investors, banks, and large market makers who provide liquidity through centralized order books. In crypto, while CeFi platforms and proprietary trading firms play a significant role in ensuring liquidity, they do not have a monopoly on the activity. This difference in market structure leads to higher price swings in crypto, as liquidity can be fragmented across various platforms and assets but also represents an opportunity.

Regulatory Environment and Risk Management

Traditional markets operate within well-established regulatory frameworks, with institutions such as the SEC, CFTC, and central banks enforcing compliance, investor protections, and anti-manipulation measures. Crypto markets, in contrast, remain largely unregulated or face differing regulations across jurisdictions. CeFi platforms often implement compliance measures similar to traditional financial institutions, while DeFi platforms operate with fewer regulatory constraints. This lack of uniformity leads to risks that will be covered later, including exchange collapses, security breaches, and smart contract exploits, all of which are less common in traditional financial markets.

Takeaways

Crypto markets are still developing, with inefficiencies such as liquidity fragmentation, regulatory uncertainty, and structural gaps creating unique risks and opportunities. Unlike traditional finance, crypto operates continuously, settles instantly, and lacks standardized oversight, contributing to its volatility. While CeFi mirrors aspects of traditional finance, DeFi introduces new financial models, further differentiating crypto from traditional markets.

3.2) The Dominance of Perpetual Futures in Crypto

Unlike traditional finance, where futures contracts with expiry dates dominate, cryptocurrency markets are led by perpetual futures, commonly known as "perps." These futures contracts, which never expire, represent the majority of crypto derivatives trading volume, with billions in daily open interest. Their structure aligns well with crypto's 24/7 market and highly speculative trading culture. This section explores why perps dominate crypto trading while traditional financial markets have not widely adopted them and how they work.

Why Perpetual Futures Dominate Crypto Markets

- **Designed for Retail Traders:** Perps cater to retail and institutional traders looking for leverage and short-term opportunities. Unlike traditional futures, perps do not require traders to manage contract expiries, making them easier to use. The availability of high leverage amplifies speculative activity, attracting traders who seek large returns from small capital investments.

- **Lack of Natural Hedgers:** In traditional finance, futures markets serve both speculative traders and natural hedgers, such as commodity producers managing price risk. However, crypto lacks significant natural hedgers that tend to prefer expiry dates that align with their needs, meaning futures are primarily used for speculation and short-term trading strategies. This fundamental difference has contributed to the dominance of perps, as traditional-style futures with expirations do not serve a strong hedging demand in crypto markets.

Funding Rate Mechanism in Perpetual Futures

Why does the price of a traditional futures contract trade at or near the price of the underlying asset since they are separate markets with separate supply and demand? The answer lies in the basis trade covered previously, an arbitrage strategy that allows participants to capture price differences with the guarantee that prices will converge at expiration when settlement happens.

Unlike traditional futures, perpetual futures never expire and there is no settlement, removing the natural convergence mechanism of expiry-based arbitrage. Arbitrageurs need to know that prices will converge for the basis trade to be viable. So, how do perp prices stay in line with spot prices? The answer lies in the funding rate mechanism, an alternative method to ensure long-term price convergence.

Traders holding positions pay or receive funding fees periodically based on whether perps are trading above or below the index price:

- If the perp price is above the index price, long traders pay short traders.

- If the perp price is below the index price, short traders pay long traders.

This system incentivizes market participants to take positions that push the perp price toward the spot price, ensuring continuous price alignment without an expiration-based settlement.

Takeaways

Perpetual futures dominate crypto markets due to their ability to provide continuous leveraged exposure without expirations. Unlike traditional futures, which rely on expiry-based arbitrage for price convergence, perps use a funding rate mechanism to maintain price alignment with spot markets. This structure fuels high volatility, frequent liquidations, and a speculative trading environment, making perps a critical component of crypto price discovery. Understanding how they function is essential for traders navigating crypto derivatives markets.

3.3) Centralized and Decentralized Finance: Two Parallel Financial Systems

Unlike traditional finance, cryptocurrency markets operate across two distinct systems: CeFi and DeFi. Both serve similar financial functions—trading, lending, borrowing, staking, and derivatives—but with fundamental differences in their structure, risks, and accessibility. While CeFi mirrors aspects of traditional finance by providing familiar user experiences and regulatory compliance, DeFi introduces smart contract-based alternatives that eliminate intermediaries. Despite their differences, CeFi and DeFi are deeply interconnected, shaping the overall crypto market landscape.

Centralized Finance: The Traditional Approach to Crypto

CeFi consists of centralized institutions such as Binance, Coinbase, and formerly FTX, which act as intermediaries facilitating financial services. These platforms operate similarly to traditional financial institutions, offering custodial trading, lending, and derivatives markets where users deposit funds with a trusted entity.

Key Characteristics:

- **Custodial Services:** Users hand over control of their assets to the platform.

- **Regulatory Compliance:** CeFi companies adhere to varying degrees of Know Your Customer (KYC)/Anti-Money Laundering (AML) regulations.

- **Fiat On/Off-Ramps:** Users can easily convert fiat to crypto and vice versa.

- **Deep Liquidity:** Centralized order books provide tighter spreads and efficient execution.

CeFi offers a user-friendly experience with seamless fiat integration, deep liquidity, and established risk controls. However, it comes with counterparty risk, potential regulatory challenges, and a lack of transparency, as seen in cases like the FTX collapse.

Decentralized Finance: The Trustless Alternative

DeFi replaces intermediaries with smart contract-based protocols, allowing users to engage in financial activities without trusting a third party. Protocols like Uniswap, Aave, and MakerDAO enable decentralized trading, lending, and stablecoin issuance, all secured by blockchain technology.

Key Characteristics:

- **Non-Custodial:** Users retain control of their private keys and funds.

- **Permissionless:** Open access without intermediaries or identity verification.

- **Composability:** Protocols integrate seamlessly, creating an open financial ecosystem.

- **Transparent Ledgers:** Transactions are publicly visible on-chain.

DeFi offers full asset control, transparency, automation, and censorship resistance, enabling a trustless financial system. However, it comes with smart contract risks, fragmented liquidity, regulatory uncertainty, and a complex user experience.

How Centralized and Decentralized Finance Interact

CeFi and DeFi may seem like separate systems, but they are closely linked. Centralized institutions leverage DeFi for yield opportunities, while DeFi depends on CeFi for liquidity and fiat on-ramps. This interplay creates a dynamic financial ecosystem where innovations and risks flow between both sectors.

- **CeFi Uses DeFi for Yield Generation:** CEXs and lending platforms deploy assets into DeFi protocols to generate yield. For example, CeFi institutions stake user deposits in liquidity pools or DeFi lending markets to enhance returns.

- **DeFi Relies on CeFi for On/Off-Ramps:** While DeFi eliminates intermediaries, it still depends on CEXs for fiat conversion. Stablecoin issuers like USDT and USDC operate in CeFi, providing liquidity that fuels DeFi activity.

- **Risk Spillover Between CeFi and DeFi:** The failure of CeFi institutions can create liquidity crises in DeFi. For example, when a major CeFi lender collapses, it can trigger mass liquidations in DeFi lending protocols. Similarly, CeFi platforms holding DeFi assets can accelerate DeFi market crashes if forced liquidations occur.

Takeaways

CeFi and DeFi represent two parallel yet interconnected financial systems within crypto markets. CeFi offers accessibility and regulatory oversight, while DeFi provides transparency and decentralization. CeFi institutions use DeFi for yield generation, while DeFi relies on CeFi for liquidity and fiat access.

4. Core Components of Decentralized Finance

This section explores the core components of DeFi, starting with DEXs, which facilitate peer-to-peer trading. It then examines money markets, which allow users to borrow and lend assets in a decentralized manner. The evolution of staking, restaking, and liquid staking derivatives (LSDs) is also covered, highlighting new ways users can earn rewards while maintaining liquidity. Finally, tokenized yield-trading is explored, showing how DeFi enables the financialization of on-chain yield opportunities.

Together, these components form the foundation of a parallel financial system, offering new opportunities but also introducing unique risks. Understanding these building blocks is crucial for the core strategies explored in this book.

4.1) Decentralized Exchanges

DEXs allow users to trade cryptocurrencies directly, without intermediaries. The most significant innovation enabling DEXs to function efficiently is the Automated Market Maker (AMM) model, which replaces traditional order books with liquidity pools. While they have their limitations, AMMs have transformed DeFi by allowing permissionless trading and broad participation in liquidity provision.

What Are Automated Market Makers?

In traditional finance, order books match buy and sell orders to determine asset prices. AMMs eliminate this model by enabling users to trade against liquidity pools instead of individual counterparties. Liquidity providers (LPs) deposit token pairs into these pools, and trades are executed automatically based on mathematical pricing formulas rather than direct market matching.

This new primitive allows anyone to launch a token without reliance on traditional market-makers to provide liquidity to the market. It democratizes the market-making role, allowing anyone to participate in providing liquidity and earning fees, rather than relying on centralized institutions or specialized trading firms.

Building blocks of AMM models:

- Constant Product Model $(x * y = k)$ – Uniswap v2
    - Maintains a balance between two assets, automatically adjusting prices as trades occur.

- Strengths: Simple, effective for general trading pairs.

- Limitations: High slippage for large trades, inefficient capital utilization.

- StableSwap Model – Curve Finance
  - Optimized for stablecoin trading, reducing slippage when assets have similar values.

  - Strengths: Highly efficient for stablecoin pairs.

- Multi-Asset Weighted Pools – Balancer
  - Allows custom asset weightings, enabling index-like liquidity pools.

  - Strengths: Greater flexibility, enabling dynamic portfolio strategies.

Why Automated Market Makers Are Revolutionary

- **Permissionless Listing:** Anyone can create and list a token without relying on centralized approval.

- **Permissionless Trading:** Anyone can swap tokens without relying on a centralized intermediary.

- **Liquidity Democratization:** Users can earn fees by providing liquidity rather than requiring institutional market makers.

- **Composability in DeFi:** AMM liquidity pools integrate seamlessly with lending, staking, and derivatives protocols, allowing assets deposited in AMMs to be leveraged across multiple financial applications.

Limitations and Risks of Automated Market Makers

- **Capital Inefficiency and Slippage:** In models such as Uniswap v2, liquidity is distributed across all price ranges, making much of it underutilized. This inefficiency results in higher slippage, as large trades can significantly impact prices due to limited liquidity concentration.

- **Exposure to Impermanent Loss:** Liquidity providers face risks when asset prices diverge. *(To be explored later in the book.)*

Together, capital inefficiency and slippage highlight a fundamental tradeoff in AMM-based trading. While AMMs enable decentralized liquidity provision, they struggle with optimizing capital usage and minimizing price impact for large trades. As a result, new models, such as concentrated liquidity, aim to improve efficiency while maintaining AMM flexibility.

Concentrated Liquidity

Traditional AMMs distribute liquidity evenly across all price ranges, leading to inefficiencies. Concentrated liquidity, introduced by Uniswap v3, allows liquidity providers to specify price ranges in which their liquidity is active. This increases capital efficiency and allows LPs to earn more fees with less capital. However, it also requires active management and comes with greater impermanent loss risks. *(This topic will be explored in depth later in the book.)*

The Emergence of Order-Book-Based Decentralized Exchanges

The reason AMMs came to exist is that blockchains lacked the throughput to support market-maker activity on order books, which led to a lack of liquidity. However, with technological advancement, blockchains are emerging that have sufficient throughput for high-frequency orders, and order-book-based DEXs are starting to emerge.

Order-book models are being adopted for improved price discovery and execution, particularly in derivatives markets. These solutions aim to merge the ethos of decentralization and self-custody with the high-quality experience of CEX-style trading. At the time of writing, Hyperliquid seems to be succeeding in capturing this market, with stability, speed, and cost matching top CEXs while allowing participants to maintain control of their assets.

Takeaways

AMMs have revolutionized DeFi by enabling liquidity pools and permissionless access, making DEXs its backbone. They allow users to trade assets seamlessly while providing opportunities for liquidity providers to earn yield. However, capital inefficiencies and exposure to impermanent loss remain major challenges, prompting innovations like concentrated liquidity and returns to order-book models. As DeFi continues to evolve, AMMs will remain a core mechanism for decentralized trading, with ongoing refinements improving their efficiency and usability.

4.2) Money Markets

Lending protocols, or money markets, are the second-largest sub-sector of DeFi by TVL, surpassed only by liquid staking. With over $45 billion locked in these protocols, they are a cornerstone of the DeFi ecosystem. Unlike traditional financial systems, DeFi money markets allow anyone to borrow or lend crypto assets without the need for credit checks, submission of personal information, or intermediaries. Borrowing and lending on these platforms is over-collateralized, ensuring that loans are backed by assets exceeding their value to mitigate risk.

This innovative financial infrastructure has enabled a range of opportunities for capital efficiency, risk management, and yield generation, making money markets a critical component of DeFi.

Basic Dynamics of Lending and Borrowing

- **Lending:** Supplying tokens to the protocol enables users to earn interest on their assets while also using the supplied tokens as collateral. Tokens deposited into the protocol automatically accrue interest based on the prevailing market supply rate. As the balance of supplied tokens grows, interest is dynamically accrued and reflects the current rate allocated to suppliers.

- **Borrowing:** Borrowing tokens from the protocol provides users with liquidity by leveraging their supplied tokens as collateral. This process allows borrowers to unlock capital without selling their assets. However, borrowers must carefully manage the risk of liquidation, which occurs if the value of their collateral compared to their debt falls below the required threshold. Borrowing interest rates are determined dynamically and accrue based on the utilization rate, representing the percentage of supplied liquidity that is borrowed.

Liquidations

Liquidation is the process that occurs when a borrower's collateral is no longer sufficient to cover its debt according to prevailing thresholds, resulting in the sale of collateral to repay part of the debt and bring the position back to a safer level.

To avoid liquidation risk, borrowers should maintain a healthy collateralization ratio, ensuring their positions remain over-collateralized even as market conditions fluctuate or interest accrues. Actively monitoring the health factor of borrow positions is crucial for mitigating risk and ensuring the security of supplied assets.

The health factor is a critical metric for assessing the safety of a borrow position in decentralized money markets. It is calculated as:

Health Factor = (Total Collateral Value * Weighted Average Liquidation Threshold) / Total Borrow Value

This metric represents the stability of a borrow position, with a health factor below 1 indicating a risk of liquidation. The liquidation threshold defines the maximum percentage of an asset's value that can be borrowed. For instance, if a user supplies $100,000 in ETH with an 80% liquidation threshold and borrows $50,000 in USDC, the health factor would be 1.6. A health factor above 1 indicates that the position remains safely above the liquidation threshold.

Monitoring the health factor is essential, as it fluctuates with changes in the value of the collateral and borrowed assets. Users can improve their health factor by supplying additional collateral or repaying part of the borrowed amount.

The appropriate target health factor depends on the volatility and correlation of the assets involved. For instance, lower health factors may be acceptable for correlated assets like stablecoins or assets closely tied to ETH. However, with volatile or uncorrelated assets, maintaining a higher health factor is prudent.

Liquidation occurs when the health factor drops below 1, meaning the collateral no longer sufficiently covers the borrowed amount. This situation can arise from a decline in collateral value or an increase in borrowed asset value. During liquidation, a portion of the borrower's debt is repaid by a liquidator, who receives a portion of the collateral in exchange. Additionally, a liquidation fee may be imposed, further reducing the borrower's remaining collateral.

Isolated Money Markets

Traditionally, money markets have operated using a single pooled model, where all assets are grouped into one lending pool. This structure shares risk across the entire protocol, meaning that if one asset in the pool becomes insolvent, the impact can ripple through the entire system. To mitigate this risk, these traditional money markets require governance approval for asset listings and parameter changes, and they enforce stringent quality requirements for listed assets. As a result, only high-quality, low-risk assets are typically permitted, limiting the flexibility and diversity of the protocol.

The limitations of pooled money markets have driven innovation toward more modular approaches, such as the isolated market model pioneered by protocols like Morpho. Isolated markets allow users to create permissionless and isolated lending markets tailored to specific asset pairs. Each market consists of:

- One loan asset
- One collateral asset
- A Liquidation Loan-to-Value (LLTV)
- An oracle for price feeds
- An interest rate model (IRM)

This framework represents a paradigm shift in money market design. By isolating risk to individual markets, these systems enable highly reactive lending and borrowing for assets of any quality without jeopardizing the entire protocol. Users can engage in lending or borrowing for niche or highly volatile assets, which would not be feasible in traditional pooled models due to systemic risk concerns.

The isolated market model greatly enhances flexibility and inclusivity in DeFi lending, fostering the growth of diverse strategies and expanding access to a broader range of assets while maintaining protocol security and resilience.

Dynamic Interest Rates

Dynamic interest rates are a defining feature of decentralized money markets, ensuring efficient allocation of capital and risk management. Borrowers pay interest on their outstanding debts, and this interest is distributed to liquidity providers (lenders) as compensation for supplying capital to the vault. A portion of the interest paid by borrowers is retained by the protocol as a fee, creating a spread between the borrowing and lending rates.

The borrowing rate of a market is determined by its interest rate model (IRM), a mathematical function that calculates the borrowing rate based on the market's utilization rate. The utilization rate represents the proportion of available assets currently borrowed.

A widely used IRM is the Linear Kink IRM. In this model, the borrowing rate increases gradually as the utilization rate rises up to a target threshold—commonly around 80%. Once the utilization exceeds this target, the borrowing rate increases sharply. This "kink" in the curve is designed to incentivize de-risking behaviors, such as additional liquidity provision or debt repayment, thereby maintaining the stability of the market.

Risks and Challenges

Borrowing and lending protocols are among the most targeted areas in DeFi, facing persistent security risks and significant financial losses. These protocols have collectively suffered an estimated $377 million in losses due to exploits and breaches.

Attack vectors on lending protocols are rather well-defined ; however, continuous development and innovation are opportunities for attackers. Understanding the most common breaches grants insight into the mechanics of lending protocols and how they work, which can be valuable in composing strategies. Major attack vectors include:

- **Oracle Price Manipulation Attacks:** A substantial number of exploits in lending protocols stem from manipulating the prices quoted by oracles. Oracles play a critical role in lending protocols, providing price data used to assess position solvency. Attackers exploit this reliance by manipulating collateral values to their advantage.

  Attackers can exploit protocols by either artificially inflating the value of collateral, thereby increasing the permissible borrowing limit, or by reducing the LTV ratio of their position to evade liquidation. Both scenarios deceive the protocol into misjudging the value of collateral or debt, resulting in significant losses.

- **Flash Loan Attacks:** Flash loans, which allow users to borrow large sums of capital within a single block without upfront collateral, are a common tool for exploits. Attackers use these loans to manipulate liquidity and exploit imbalances within protocols that fail to account for sudden spikes in capital. This leads to erroneous pricing or calculations, creating opportunities for manipulation.

- **Attacks Involving Admin Controls:** Many protocols rely on privileged accounts, often referred to as "admin keys," to manage critical functions such as upgrades, parameter adjustments, or governance decisions. If compromised, these accounts can be used to drain funds, redirect transactions, or deploy malicious contract updates disguised as legitimate protocol changes.

Delta-Neutral Applications

Money markets play a pivotal role in supporting various strategies within DeFi, including delta-neutral strategies. Money markets can be leveraged in three ways, which will be explored in depth in the lending strategies section:

- **Access to Leverage:** Money markets enable users to borrow against their collateral, providing access to leverage that can be used to amplify returns and execute trading strategies.

- **Hedging:** Borrowing an asset through a money market and selling it creates an effective hedging mechanism, as the borrower generates a profit if the borrowed token's price falls, mimicking a short position. This dynamic allows borrowing to offset a strategy's exposure to the borrowed asset.

- **Yield from Lending:** In some cases, money markets themselves serve as a source of yield. Users can lend their assets to earn interest while employing other capital-efficient techniques to manage risk and maintain neutrality.

Takeaways

DeFi money markets allow users to lend and borrow without intermediaries, using smart contracts to manage liquidity and risk. Access to this primitive enables leverage, hedging, and yield generation, which are essential tools for executing delta-neutral strategies effectively on-chain. The use of these tools will be explored in more depth in *Chapter 4: Core Strategies*.

4.3) Staking, Restaking, and Liquid Derivatives

Staking is a fundamental mechanism in Proof-of-Stake (PoS) blockchains, ensuring network security and decentralization by incentivizing participants to lock up tokens in exchange for rewards. Unlike traditional finance, where security and governance rely on centralized entities, staking distributes network validation across participants. However, traditional staking comes with limitations such as liquidity lockups, withdrawal delays, and slashing risks. To address these challenges, liquid staking derivatives (LSDs) and restaking have emerged, enabling users to enhance capital efficiency in DeFi.

How Staking Works

Validators secure the network by locking up tokens to process transactions and maintain blockchain integrity. In return, they receive staking rewards composed of newly issued tokens (inflationary rewards) and transaction fees. Since operating a validator requires technical expertise and infrastructure, many users participate in delegated staking, where they stake through validators while maintaining ownership of their funds.

Challenges of Traditional Staking

Staked assets remain illiquid while locked, preventing their use in DeFi and other financial activities. Additionally, PoS networks impose withdrawal delays, requiring users to wait for an unstaking period before regaining access to their assets. This delay can range from days to weeks, limiting flexibility and making it difficult to react to market conditions. These constraints create inefficiency in capital use, restricting the broader participation of stakers in DeFi strategies.

Liquid Staking

Liquid staking protocols solve staking's liquidity problem by issuing LSDs, which represent staked assets. These LSDs, such as stETH (Lido) or rETH (Rocket Pool), allow users to earn staking rewards while retaining liquidity, making them useful for DeFi applications.

How LSDs Enhance DeFi Strategies:

- **Collateralization:** LSDs can be used as collateral in lending markets (e.g., Aave, Compound), unlocking additional yield opportunities.

- **Leveraged Staking:** Users can borrow against their LSDs and reinvest in staking, amplifying returns.

- **Yield Composability:** LSDs integrate with yield farms and automated DeFi strategies, compounding earnings beyond standard staking rewards.

Risks of Liquid Staking:

- **Centralization Risks:** The dominance of a few liquid staking providers (e.g., Lido) raises concerns over validator centralization.

- **Smart Contract Vulnerabilities:** LSDs depend on smart contract security, exposing users to potential exploits.

- **Depegging Risks:** LSDs may trade below their underlying value due to market fluctuations or withdrawal constraints.

Restaking

EigenLayer introduced restaking in 2021, allowing users to extend the utility of their staked ETH by securing additional validation services beyond Ethereum—this mechanism is known as *pooled security*. By opting into this system, participants enable their staked assets to secure multiple protocols while receiving additional incentives. However, this comes with stricter slashing conditions, enforced by EigenLayer through control over withdrawal rights of the staked ETH.

Validators who participate in restaking benefit from higher yields, as they receive extra rewards from the actively validated services (AVSs) they support. This structure creates a market for pooled security, where protocols can access additional network security, while users can boost their staking rewards by committing to securing multiple services.

Despite these advantages, direct restaking via EigenLayer requires a minimum deposit of 32 ETH and lacks liquidity. This means that once assets are restaked, they cannot be easily withdrawn or traded. To address this, in a similar way to LSTs, several liquid restaked token (LRT) solutions have emerged.

Liquid Restaked Tokens

As LSDs enabled traditional staking, liquid restaked tokens (LRTs) provide liquidity and accessibility to restaked positions. LRTs like EtherFi's eETH, KelpDAO's rsETH, and Renzo's ezETH allow users to receive liquid tokens that represent their staked assets. These LRTs can be freely traded, used as collateral, or deployed in various DeFi strategies while still earning restaking rewards.

Similar to LSDs, LRTs ensure that users maintain access to their capital while participating in restaking. They unlock greater capital efficiency, enabling users to integrate their restaked positions into lending, borrowing, and trading strategies within the DeFi ecosystem. As adoption grows, LRTs are poised to become a fundamental component of on-chain financial infrastructure.

Takeaways

Staking plays a critical role in securing PoS blockchains, but traditional staking locks up liquidity, limiting its usability in DeFi. LSDs solve this problem by enabling DeFi composability, allowing users to earn staking rewards while maintaining liquidity. Restaking expands staking utility even further, offering enhanced yield but also introducing new slashing and centralization risks. As DeFi evolves, LSDs and restaking will continue shaping the next phase of capital-efficient staking strategies.

4.4) Tokenized Yield-Trading

The interest derivatives market is one of the largest financial sectors globally, with over $550 trillion in notional value in 2023. It plays a crucial role in traditional finance by enabling the trading and hedging of interest rate exposure. These instruments provide essential tools for risk management, liquidity, and capital efficiency, making them indispensable for sophisticated investors.

Tokenized yield-trading platforms bring these sophisticated financial tools into DeFi by enabling users to tokenize and trade future yields. These platforms split yield-bearing assets into two components: the principal and the yield, enabling these new possibilities.

How Yield Tokenization Works

A *yield-bearing token* is an umbrella term that refers to any token that generates yield. For example:

- Liquid staked assets such as Lido's stETH and wstETH
- Liquid restaked assets such as EtherFi's weETH
- Liquid staked stablecoins such as Ethena's sUSDe
- Liquidity provider tokens such as Uniswap LP tokens

Yield tokenization allows a yield-bearing asset to be divided into:

- **Principal Token (PT):** Represents the ownership of the underlying asset, akin to a zero-coupon bond.
- **Yield Token (YT):** Represents claims on the yield generated by the asset until maturity, akin to detached bond coupons.

This concept mirrors the traditional finance process of bond stripping, where a bond's principal and interest are separated into tradable components.

Note that the underlying asset being divided into the PT and YT tokens implies the PT and YT can be combined at any time to recreate the underlying asset.

To better illustrate this, we can look at the example of a real estate property—it is a yield-bearing asset—that generates rental yield to the owner of the property.

Consider a real estate property that's been split into two components:

- The rights to the ownership of the property. This can be seen as the PT.

- The rights to the rental income of the property, which can grant its owner the right to collect all the rental income (yield) generated by the property for a certain length of time. This can be seen as the YT.

It makes sense that at any point in time, both can be combined to get the whole property.

Relative Asset Pricing

All of these components have a clear relationship, and their prices are interconnected. The most important equation for valuing tokenized yield assets is the following:

PT Price + YT Price = Underlying Asset Price

As demonstrated in the equation above, the combined price of PT and YT should equate to the price of the underlying asset as they're individual parts of a whole. On maturity, PT can be redeemed for its underlying without its YT counterpart, as explained below.

Prices of PTs and YTs fluctuate based on supply and demand as a result of market speculation about future yields. The balance between PT and YT prices to add up to the underlying asset price reflects the agreed-upon yield of the asset according to the market—*the implied yield*.

Looking back at the equation above, it explains why PT tokens are redeemable for the underlying asset at maturity without their YT counterpart:

The YT price is the market's best estimate of yields that will be generated until maturity, so as the YT approaches maturity, there is less and less yield left to be generated, so naturally, the YT price approaches 0. At maturity, there are no more yields to be generated, so the YT token is worth 0. Consequently, PT Price = Underlying Asset Price.

Understanding this relationship and balance is critical to appreciating how PT and YT prices reflect the market's view on future yields of an asset.

In Practice, Where Does Principal Token Yield Come From?

The relative pricing equation can be rearranged as such:

PT Price = Underlying Asset Price - YT Price

As shown, the higher the future yield is estimated to be (YT price), the lower the price of the principal (PT price) relative to the entire Underlying Asset Price.

The lower the price of the principal (PT) relative to the Underlying Asset Price, the larger the discount and, therefore, the larger the implied yield, since it will be redeemable 1:1 for the underlying asset at maturity.

Let's get back to the rental property example. Say the maturity date is in one year:

Assuming the current price of the property is *$100,000 and the market* estimates that the property will yield $10,000 during this year, the price of the PT is $90,000 *($90,000 + $10,000 = $100,000).*

You can buy the rights to ownership for the property at a lower price than the actual property. After one year, the rights entitle you to redeem the property.

The guaranteed value appreciation from the discounted value of paper ownership to owning the property at its full value constitutes the fixed yield/income.

In summary:

- PT lets you redeem the underlying principal asset after the maturity date.

- PT has a lower entry cost than the original asset. PT value grows over time and becomes 1:1 redeemable with the original asset at maturity.

- You earn a fixed yield by buying and holding PT. The difference between the entry cost and the redemption value is your fixed yield.

- PT is similar to zero-coupon bonds in traditional finance.

In Practice, Where Does Yield Token Yield Come From?

Inversely, you can also buy only the yield portion (YT) to receive rent for one year. Still assuming the market estimates the property will yield $10,000 this year, the YT price is $10,000. You'll profit when you collect more than $10,000 within the year or suffer a loss when it yields less. As you can see, YTs can lead to realized losses contrary to PTs, which can only leave gains on the table (by locking a fixed yield below the actual yield generated by maturity).

In summary:

- YT lets you receive the yield of the underlying asset until its maturity date, claimable in real time.

- By buying YT, you can gain exposure to just the yield at a much lower price than the principal. You profit if the yield you receive is more than what you paid for the YT.

- The much lower price compared to the entire asset allows you to get leveraged yield exposure without liquidation or oracle risk.

- YT is similar to detached coupons of bonds in traditional finance.

Accounting Assets

The accounting asset is the asset against which the yield-bearing token appreciates in value. While some tokens have a clear accounting asset, others do not. Upon maturity, PTs can be redeemed 1:1 for the accounting asset.

Understanding the distinction between accounting assets and base assets is essential for accurately valuing the expected payouts of PTs. The difference between the accounting asset and the base asset introduces a critical nuance in determining payouts.

Yield-bearing tokens fall into two categories:

- **Rebasing Assets:** Tokens such as stETH or GLP accrue yield by increasing the token count or balance over time. For example, if you hold 1 stETH and earn a 10% yield, your balance will increase to 1.1 stETH, which is worth 1.1 ETH. The accounting asset for these tokens is themselves, as their value remains equal to the base asset.

- **Interest-Bearing Assets:** Tokens like ezETH or cDAI accrue yield by increasing in value relative to their base asset (e.g., ETH for ezETH and DAI for cDAI). For instance, if you hold 1 ezETH (worth 1 ETH) and earn a 10% yield, your balance will remain 1 ezETH, but its value has increased to 1.1 ETH. For these tokens, the accounting asset is the base asset to avoid double-counting yield.

The distinction between rebasing and interest-bearing tokens is well illustrated by comparing stETH and wstETH. While stETH is rebasing, wstETH is interest-bearing. As a result, at the time of writing, 1 stETH ≈ 0.84 wstETH, reflecting the accrued yield captured by the interest-bearing version.

This difference has important implications for PTs. For rebasing assets, the accounting asset is the token itself, while for interest-bearing assets, the accounting asset is the base asset. In some cases, it can greatly affect payout calculations, as shown in this example:

The value of ezETH increases over time relative to ETH as staking and restaking rewards accrue. Upon maturity, 1 PT-ezETH is redeemable for 1 ETH worth of ezETH, not 1 ezETH, which would be worth more than 1 ETH due to its accrued value. Understanding this nuance is critical to accurately assessing expected payouts and avoiding miscalculations in yield-bearing strategies.

Takeaways

Yield-trading platforms unlock a new frontier for DeFi, allowing sophisticated strategies and attracting institutional capital by enabling hedging and speculation on yields, as well as improved liquidity management. By enabling advanced financial tools in a decentralized environment, these platforms represent a critical step forward for the maturation of the DeFi market.

5. Stablecoins

Stablecoins are a core component of crypto, designed to maintain a stable value by pegging to fiat currencies or other assets. Unlike volatile cryptocurrencies, they provide price stability, making them essential for trading, payments, and financial applications.

Introduced in 2014 with Tether (USDT), stablecoins saw explosive growth, especially during DeFi Summer in 2020, when they became integral to lending, borrowing, and liquidity in DeFi. Their clear market fit led to widespread adoption, with supply surging from $5 billion in 2019 to over $150 billion in 2021.

Today, stablecoins serve as a unit of account, store of value, and medium of exchange, enabling efficient capital deployment and reducing transaction costs. The following sections will explore their types, mechanisms, and risks.

5.1) Definition, Role, and Use Cases in Markets

Stablecoins are cryptocurrencies designed to maintain a stable value by pegging to an external asset, such as fiat currency (e.g., USD) or commodities (e.g., gold). They achieve stability through collateralization (backed by reserves) or algorithmic mechanisms that regulate supply and demand.

They play a vital role in the crypto ecosystem by offering price stability in an otherwise volatile market. Their predictable value makes them indispensable for trading, DeFi applications, and everyday transactions.

Unit of Account

Stablecoins serve as a standard pricing benchmark across most CEXs and DEXs. By providing a stable, on-chain value to measure asset prices against, they improve the efficiency and ease of use of cryptocurrency markets.

Store of Value

During periods of high volatility, stablecoins provide a safe haven for traders and investors without the friction of converting funds back into a fiat currency. They also support DeFi applications, enabling lending, borrowing, and other activities with fiat currency equivalents, and thus allowing users to easily participate in DeFi without being exposed to crypto assets' volatility.

Medium of Exchange

Stablecoins facilitate fast, low-cost transactions, making them a preferred option for global payments and remittances. Their ability to bypass traditional banking fees and delays has driven their adoption in cross-border financial transactions.

By serving as a bridge between traditional finance and digital assets, stablecoins have become a cornerstone of crypto markets. The next section explores the different types of stablecoins and their unique mechanisms.

5.2) Types of Stablecoins

Stablecoins differ in their collateral backing and stabilization mechanisms, shaping their decentralization, scalability, and risk profile. Their design dictates how they maintain their peg and withstand market volatility.

Fiat-Backed Stablecoins (e.g., USDC, USDT)

These stablecoins are fully backed by reserves held in traditional financial institutions. Their peg is maintained through direct redemption mechanisms, allowing users to exchange them for fiat at a 1:1 ratio. While highly liquid and widely adopted, they are centralized and subject to regulatory oversight. Additionally, issuers generate substantial profits from their reserves, which are not shared with users.

Commodity-Backed Stablecoins (e.g., XAUT, PAXG)

Backed by physical assets like gold, these stablecoins provide exposure to commodities while benefiting from blockchain efficiency. Their peg is maintained via a redemption mechanism, allowing users to exchange tokens for the underlying asset. They depend on trusted custodians for asset backing.

Collateralized Debt Position Stablecoins (e.g., USDS, GHO)

Collateralized debt positions (CDPs) refer to stablecoins minted by locking collateral in a smart contract. These stablecoins function as system-issued debt, requiring robust mechanisms to maintain their peg. Established oracle infrastructures ensure accurate valuations of collateral and debt at all times.

Crypto-backed CDP stablecoins require over-collateralization due to the volatility of their underlying assets. Stability mechanisms vary across protocols, incorporating redemption models, interest rate adjustments, and dynamic borrowing costs to regulate supply and demand.

Delta-Neutral Stablecoins (e.g., USDe, USR)

These stablecoins utilize delta-neutral strategies to maintain a stable value. The protocol takes collateral representing a spot long position and hedges it through perpetual short positions. This structure keeps the asset's value steady while generating yield from funding rates and staking rewards, enabling the issuance of stablecoins backed by hedged positions. The staking interest rate is determined by yield generation, while peg stability relies on arbitrage and redemption mechanisms. The primary risk lies in the custody and execution of hedging positions.

Each stablecoin type presents trade-offs between decentralization, stability, and regulatory exposure. The next section will explore how stablecoin interest rates interconnect across DeFi markets.

5.3) Interconnectivity of Stablecoin Rates

Stablecoin interest rates are deeply interconnected across DeFi markets, influencing borrowing, lending, and minting dynamics. Fluctuations in leading rates create arbitrage opportunities that drive liquidity shifts and impact the broader ecosystem.

Stablecoin Mint/Borrow Rate Correlation via Carry Trades

Differences in stablecoin minting and borrowing rates naturally create arbitrage opportunities. For example, if the GHO borrow rate is 8% while Maker's Sky Savings Rate (SSR) is 12.5%, informed participants will borrow GHO, sell it for USDS, and stake USDS to earn the higher yield, generating a 4.5% spread. This selling pressure on GHO causes it to depeg downward, forcing governance to adjust mint rates to restore equilibrium and eliminate the arbitrage.

Structural Carry Trade Products Magnify Rate Convergence

Platforms like Morpho and Euler, facilitated by protocols such as Contango, enable leveraged stablecoin carry trades. Users can loop stablecoins against each other, amplifying interest rate arbitrage and accelerating rate alignment across markets. These leveraged strategies drive liquidity toward the highest-yielding stablecoins, reinforcing systemic rate convergence.

Delayed Rate Response from Collateralized Debt Positions

The market interest rates tend to align with a benchmark. The benchmark rate, such as SSR, leads rate movements by setting a reference point for other assets to position relative to, depending on their risk profile. When arbitrageurs sell CDP stablecoins (e.g., GHO) to fund higher-yielding alternatives, peg strain forces them to adjust mint and borrow rates in response. These adjustments typically lag behind real-time market conditions, creating step-change effects in money supply. This dynamic mirrors traditional monetary policy mechanisms, such as those employed by the US Federal Reserve, where delayed responses to liquidity demand can cause abrupt market shifts.

Takeaways

Stablecoin rates do not operate in isolation; they are dynamically linked through arbitrage and liquidity shifts. Rate inefficiencies create opportunities for profit but also shape broader DeFi rate structures, reinforcing systemic interconnectivity.

5.4) Stablecoin Trilemma: Security, Scalability, and Decentralization

Stablecoins have become a cornerstone of the crypto ecosystem, but their designs come with inherent risks and trade-offs. They face a similar trilemma as blockchains between security, scalability, and decentralization, which introduces systemic vulnerabilities that market participants must carefully consider.

The Stablecoin Trilemma: Security, Scalability, and Decentralization

Stablecoins must balance three fundamental properties:

- **Security:** Protection against external attacks and systemic failures.

- **Scalability:** Capacity to support large-scale adoption and transaction volumes.

- **Decentralization:** Ensuring no single entity has control over issuance and management.

No stablecoin design optimally achieves all three. Trade-offs can lead to significant vulnerabilities, as seen in the collapse of Terra's UST, which sacrificed security for an unsustainable peg mechanism, and BUSD's regulatory-induced decline, highlighting the risks of centralization.

Algorithmic Stablecoins and the Definition Debate

A growing debate questions whether all so-called stablecoins should be classified as such. Some, like delta-neutral stablecoins (e.g., USDe, USR), function more like interest-bearing vault tokens than traditional fiat-backed stablecoins. Unlike USDC or USDT, which are redeemable 1:1 for fiat, delta-neutral stablecoins derive their value from hedged positions, making them subject to market fluctuations and strategy-based risks.

Regulatory and Centralization Risks

Fiat-backed stablecoins are especially susceptible to regulatory intervention. BUSD's rapid supply reduction following US regulatory scrutiny exemplifies how centralized oversight can impact their circulation. Meanwhile, over-collateralized and algorithmic stablecoins aim to mitigate regulatory dependence but often struggle with scalability or maintaining consistent peg stability.

Takeaways

Stablecoins are not without risk. Their structural differences lead to varying levels of decentralization, security, and scalability trade-offs. Understanding these nuances is crucial for users engaging in DeFi strategies, as stablecoin risks extend beyond simple peg stability to include regulatory threats, governance centralization, and underlying collateral volatility.

Chapter 3: Foundations of Delta-Neutral Strategies

Delta-neutral strategies enable traders to profit from market inefficiencies while minimizing exposure to directional price movements. By structuring positions that balance long and short exposures, these strategies reduce volatility and allow for stable returns regardless of market trends.

This chapter explores the core principles of delta-neutral trading, beginning with risk management fundamentals, diversification strategies, and the role of hedging in capital efficiency. It then delves into the mechanics of delta-neutral positioning, identifying market inefficiencies and applying risk controls to sustain long-term profitability. Mastering these concepts is essential for effectively executing delta-neutral strategies in both traditional and cryptocurrency markets.

1. Understanding and Managing Risk

Financial markets operate as probabilistic systems where no participant has perfect information. Every trade or investment involves uncertainty, making risk management just as important as profit maximization. While participants aim to maximize EV, they must also manage variance—the degree to which returns fluctuate. Without proper risk management, even a strategy with a strong EV can fail due to excessive volatility and unsustainable drawdowns.

Delta-neutral strategies incorporate risk management by design, as they aim to eliminate directional exposure and focus on capturing predictable inefficiencies rather than speculative gains. By maintaining a neutral position, these strategies control variance, stabilize returns, and enhance capital efficiency, allowing traders to scale with confidence while minimizing exposure to market fluctuations.

This section explores the key risk factors affecting delta-neutral strategies, including market risk, liquidity risk, counterparty risk, and systemic risk. It also introduces essential risk measurement tools and management techniques, equipping traders with the knowledge to construct robust, resilient strategies that withstand market fluctuations.

1.1) Types of Risk in Financial Markets

Many traders assume that neutralizing price exposure removes all risk, yet numerous non-directional risks can still threaten capital. Risk factors, such as liquidity constraints, counterparty failures, operational errors, and systemic shocks, remain critical concerns for delta-neutral strategies.

While this is not an exhaustive list, the risks outlined below are among the most significant. These risks often interact, meaning that a failure in one area can amplify exposure to another. Understanding them is crucial for building a resilient, risk-adjusted strategy.

Market Risk: Residual Exposure Beyond Delta Neutrality

Even after eliminating directional price exposure, traders remain vulnerable to residual market risks, including:

- **Hedge Imperfections:** Miscalculations or structural inefficiencies can create unintended price exposure.

- **Volatility Spikes:** Sudden increases in volatility can lead to wider bid-ask spreads, higher slippage, and unexpected liquidations.

For example, a funding rate arbitrage trader without a strong monitoring system may suddenly be liquidated on one side of the trade due to extraordinary volatility, incurring a loss.

Liquidity Risk: The Challenge of Trade Execution

Liquidity risk arises when an asset cannot be bought or sold efficiently without excessive price impact. Even in delta-neutral strategies, liquidity constraints can introduce new risks:

- **Execution Liquidity Risk:** Large position sizes can move the market against the trader, reducing expected profitability.

- **Market-Wide Liquidity Crises:** During extreme volatility, liquidity providers may withdraw from markets, making it difficult to exit positions.

- **Cross-Exchange Fragmentation:** Arbitrage strategies rely on moving capital between platforms, but withdrawal delays or fragmented liquidity can prevent timely rebalancing.

For example, a trader arbitraging funding rates on Binance and a DEX experiences unexpected withdrawal freezes, leaving them temporarily unable to rebalance their position while the price is moving against one of the positions, requiring more margin.

Counterparty Risk: Centralized and Decentralized Finance Failures

Counterparty risk refers to the possibility that a trading venue, lending protocol, liquidity provider, or other counterparty fails to meet its obligations. This is a major concern in both CeFi and DeFi environments:

- **CeFi Counterparty Risks:** CEXs may face regulatory shutdown or become insolvent (e.g., FTX collapse, 2022).

- **DeFi Counterparty Risks:** Protocols can be exploited through attack vectors, such as smart contract vulnerabilities or oracle manipulation, leading to total loss of funds.

For example, a trader using on-chain lending markets as a hedge loses their collateral when the protocol is exploited, despite their position being delta-neutral.

Operational Risk: Execution Errors, Human Mistakes, and System Failures

Operational risk encompasses errors in execution, system failures, or security lapses. Common operational risks include:

- **Trade Execution Mistakes:** Miscalculating order size, leverage, or hedge ratios.

- **Automation and Bot Failures:** Algorithmic strategies that fail to rebalance positions due to technical issues.

- **Security Breaches:** Phishing attacks, leaked API keys, or compromised wallets can result in unauthorized transactions and loss of funds.

For example, a trader relying on an automated delta-hedging bot fails to notice that API errors prevent the bot from adjusting positions, leading to unhedged exposure.

Systemic Risk: Market-Wide Disruptions That Affect All Strategies

Systemic risk refers to events that trigger broad market instability, making even well-structured delta-neutral strategies vulnerable. Examples include:

- **Stablecoin Depegging:** Events like USDC's temporary depeg in 2023 can cause mass liquidations in lending protocols.

- **Cascading Liquidations:** One major liquidation event can trigger a domino effect across trading venues.

- **Regulatory Crackdowns:** Government actions that ban or restrict trading platforms can limit access and disrupt liquidity.

For example, a participant using a DeFi lending platform to earn yield via a looped stablecoin position gets liquidated due to USDC depegging.

Takeaways

Delta-neutral strategies are not risk-free—while removing price exposure significantly reduces return variance, it does not eliminate the dangers posed by liquidity constraints, counterparty failures, operational errors, and systemic risks. Traders must recognize that these risks are often interconnected, meaning that a failure in one area can cascade into significant losses. Proper risk assessment, monitoring, and mitigation strategies are essential to ensure long-term sustainability in delta-neutral trading.

1.2) Why Risk Management Is Crucial

Delta-neutral strategies aim to isolate market inefficiencies by eliminating directional market risk, commonly the largest source of volatility for a strategy. However, no strategy is risk-free—delta-neutral trading still carries risks that, if not properly managed, can lead to substantial losses.

Many traders, particularly in the cryptocurrency space, underestimate the impact of risk management. While a strategy may be structurally sound, poor risk control can erase otherwise consistent profits in a single unexpected event. Risk management is not about maximizing gains—it is about ensuring survival and capital growth over time.

The Asymmetric Nature of Losses

A core reason why risk management is paramount is the nonlinear nature of losses. Losses are asymmetric—the deeper the drawdown, the harder it is to recover:

- A 10% loss requires only an 11.1% gain to break even.

- A 50% loss requires a 100% gain to recover.

- An 80% loss requires a 400% return to restore initial capital.

The higher the drawdown, the exponentially harder recovery becomes. This is why avoiding large drawdowns is far more important than chasing high returns. A trader with a steady, low-volatility 10% annual return will outperform another with a highly volatile strategy that suffers deep periodic losses.

Reducing Variance Is More Important Than Maximizing Returns

Even if a strategy has a positive EV, high volatility can lead to ruin before the edge materializes. When running a strategy with high volatility, capital depletion can prevent a trader from executing enough trades to let probability play out.

Consider two strategies:

- Strategy A has a 10% average annual return with low variance.

- Strategy B has a 20% average annual return but suffers a 40% drawdown every few years.

Strategy A's lower-variance enables better capital efficiency, allowing traders to leverage up and generate even higher absolute returns than Strategy B while being exposed to less risk of ruin.

Delta-Neutral Strategies Negate One Type of Risk, but Not All

While delta-neutral strategies neutralize exposure to price fluctuations, they do not eliminate risk altogether. Other risks remain, including:

- **Liquidity Risk:** The inability to exit positions efficiently without high slippage.

- **Counterparty Risk:** Exchange insolvencies, smart contract vulnerabilities, or other counterparty defaults.

- **Operational Risk:** Execution errors, automation failures, or security breaches.

- **Systemic Risk:** Black swan events, stablecoin depegging, or regulatory shocks.

For example, a trader engaged in funding rate arbitrage might successfully neutralize price risk but remain exposed to sudden exchange withdrawal freezes or smart contract exploits.

Takeaways

Risk management is the foundation of long-term success for all financial strategies, including delta-neutral portfolios. Managing drawdowns is more important than chasing high returns, as large losses require exponentially greater gains to recover. A low-variance strategy can be leveraged more effectively, allowing for higher returns with a lower risk of ruin. Delta-neutral strategies remove price exposure but do not eliminate other risks, such as liquidity, counterparty, operational, and systemic risks. The most sustainable traders prioritize capital preservation, enabling them to stay in the game long enough to benefit from compounding returns.

1.3) Measuring and Quantifying Risk

Risk cannot be effectively managed unless it is measured. Many traders underestimate their exposure simply because they lack structured risk assessment tools. The following metrics provide a quantifiable framework for assessing and managing these risks, ensuring that traders can make informed decisions about portfolio exposure.

Maximum Drawdown: Historical Worst Case

Maximum drawdown (MDD) represents the largest peak-to-trough loss experienced by a strategy over a given period. It provides insight into the potential capital at risk in extreme conditions and highlights the sustainability of a trading strategy.

For example, Strategy A generates an annual return of 20% but experiences a MDD of 60%, making it highly volatile. In contrast, Strategy B has a lower annual return of 10% but maintains a significantly lower drawdown of 15%, indicating greater stability. Despite lower returns, Strategy B provides more efficient capital management and reduced exposure to extreme losses.

Value at Risk: Probabilistic Worst Case

Value at Risk (VaR) estimates the maximum potential loss over a specific period with a given confidence level. There are multiple variations of VaR, each utilizing different methodologies to assess risk exposure, whether by analyzing historical data, simulating market scenarios, or relying on statistical assumptions.

For example, a 95% daily VaR of $10,000 indicates that, with 95% certainty, losses will not exceed $10,000 in a single day, though there remains a 5% probability of greater losses.

Sharpe Ratio: Risk-Adjusted Performance Metrics

The Sharpe ratio measures a portfolio's return relative to its risk. It is calculated as:

$$Sharpe\ Ratio = (PortfolioReturns - RiskFreeRate) / PortfolioVolatility$$

Portfolio Volatility is measured in standard deviations. A higher Sharpe ratio indicates better risk-adjusted returns.

For example, Strategy A has a Sharpe ratio of 1.5, meaning it generates 1.5x return per unit of risk taken, whereas Strategy B has a Sharpe ratio of 0.8, indicating weaker returns relative to volatility. Strategies with a higher Sharpe ratio are preferable, as they offer better returns relative to risk.

Stress Testing: Accounting for Tail Risks

Tail risk refers to rare events that can severely impact portfolio performance, while black swan events are highly unpredictable crises, such as the COVID-19 market crash in 2020. By definition, tail risks fall outside normal distributions, making them difficult to quantify, yet they drive the most significant market disruptions. Traditional models often underestimate their frequency and impact.

Despite this uncertainty, incorporating stress testing for extreme conditions, maintaining emergency liquidity reserves, and reducing leverage during volatility help mitigate exposure to these unpredictable but consequential events.

Takeaways

Quantifying risk is crucial for ensuring long-term sustainability in delta-neutral strategies. Metrics such as MDD, VaR, and risk-adjusted ratios help traders identify potential losses and optimize their strategies accordingly. Additionally, accounting for tail risks through stress testing allows traders to mitigate extreme events. A well-measured risk strategy enhances capital efficiency and ensures survival, even in volatile market conditions.

2. The Role of Diversification in Risk Management

Diversification is one of the most effective tools for reducing risk in portfolios. By spreading exposure across multiple independent positions, traders can limit their reliance on any single outcome, making returns more predictable and reducing the risk of ruin. In delta-neutral strategies, diversification plays a crucial role in further stabilizing returns and improving capital efficiency.

This section explores the fundamental principles of diversification, including its impact on risk reduction, the dangers of false diversification, and how traders can construct well-balanced portfolios. Mastering these concepts ensures that traders optimize their risk-adjusted returns and enhance the sustainability of their delta-neutral strategies.

2.1) Understanding the Limits of Probability

In financial markets, probability is often used as a guide for decision-making, helping traders evaluate risk and expected outcomes. However, as Howard Marks points out, probability does not dictate reality—it merely outlines possible futures. In practice, we do not experience an entire distribution of outcomes; we experience only one.

This distinction is crucial because financial markets do not operate under conditions of repeated, independent trials like rolling a die. Instead, each market event is unique, shaped by path dependency and external influences that make past probabilities an unreliable predictor of individual outcomes.

We Live in the Sample

Probability models estimate multiple potential outcomes, but in reality, only one unfolds. An 80% chance of success for a trade does not mean any single trade will necessarily succeed—rather, it implies that over numerous attempts, success should occur at that rate.

The sequence and context of events play a crucial role in determining market outcomes. Unlike casino games, where each roll is independent, financial markets are influenced by prior price movements, liquidity conditions, macroeconomic factors, and trader positioning. The order and nature of events matter just as much as probability itself.

For example, a trader may backtest a strategy and observe a historically high win rate. However, when applied in live markets, unforeseen factors such as sudden volatility, shifts in liquidity, or unexpected macroeconomic developments can cause outcomes to deviate significantly from the expected statistical probability.

Implications for Risk Management

- **Probability Alone Is Not Enough:** Traders often mistake high-probability outcomes for guarantees, failing to account for the fact that they are only experiencing a single realization of a probability model.

- **Scenario Planning Is Essential:** Because traders do not get infinite repetitions, preparing for extreme cases is as important as optimizing for likely ones.

- **Survival Over Optimization:** A strategy with an 80% success rate may still fail four or five times in a row, wiping out capital before the edge plays out. Risk-adjusted thinking prioritizes staying in the game over maximizing potential gains.

Takeaway

Probability models provide useful insights, but traders must recognize that markets do not follow clean statistical distributions. In reality, only one path unfolds, and external factors can override statistical expectations. Survival in trading is about managing risk, not assuming probabilities will always play out as expected. Traders should prioritize risk control, scenario planning, and resilience over blind reliance on statistical probabilities.

2.2) Why Diversification Matters

Diversification is one of the most effective ways to reduce risk and stabilize returns in financial markets. While it does not guarantee profits, it helps minimize exposure to extreme losses by spreading risk across multiple independent opportunities. The key principle is that by increasing the number of independent outcomes, a trader tightens returns around the EV, reducing overall variance, therefore increasing capital efficiency.

As Howard Marks highlights, we only experience one realization of the probability distribution in the real world. This means that even if a strategy has a high probability of success, it can still fail due to unique market conditions. Diversification helps counteract this by increasing reliability across different trades and reducing exposure to singular catastrophic events.

The Role of Diversification in Reducing Risk of Ruin

Since traders only experience a single path of market outcomes, diversification ensures that no single adverse event can completely derail a strategy. Increasing independent trades enhances statistical reliability, reducing the likelihood of major drawdowns.

For example, a trader who relies solely on lending in a single DeFi protocol may face severe losses if the protocol experiences a liquidity crunch, a smart contract exploit, or an unexpected regulatory intervention. In contrast, a trader who employs multiple uncorrelated strategies is less vulnerable to a single market shift, as other trades may still perform well even if one fails. This principle applies across all asset classes and trading methodologies.

How Diversification Tightens Returns Around the Expected Value

Diversification increases the number of independent trades, ensuring that returns align more closely with their EV over time. By incorporating a greater number of independent outcomes, diversification makes returns statistically more reliable, reducing unexpected deviations. This tightening effect stabilizes returns and enhances predictability, which is crucial for long-term capital growth. A key advantage is that lower variance allows for more efficient use of capital. A trader with a low-variance strategy can apply leverage more effectively while maintaining a manageable risk profile.

Takeaways

Diversification is an essential risk management tool that stabilizes returns and helps reduce the likelihood of catastrophic losses. By increasing the number of independent trades, traders create a more stable, predictable return profile and push the risk of ruin more standard deviations away. However, diversification is only effective when it truly reduces correlation and concentration risks. Simply holding multiple assets or participating in multiple strategies does not guarantee meaningful risk reduction. Traders must carefully analyze correlations and risk segmentation to avoid hidden exposures and ensure real diversification.

2.3) Avoiding False Diversification

Many traders assume they are diversified simply because they hold multiple assets or deploy multiple strategies. However, true diversification is only achieved when risk exposures are uncorrelated. False diversification occurs when traders believe they have spread their risk, but in reality, their positions remain highly interconnected. Understanding the difference between real and false diversification is critical to avoiding systemic losses.

Highly Correlated Holdings

Owning multiple assets does not automatically provide diversification if they move together under similar market conditions.

For example, a trader holds BTC, ETH, and SOL, believing they are diversified. However, cryptocurrencies are highly correlated, especially on the downside. If the crypto market crashes, all three assets will likely decline simultaneously, exposing the trader to the same market risk.

Strategy Overlap

Running multiple trading strategies that rely on the same market inefficiency can create hidden risk concentration.

For example, a trader executes funding rate arbitrage across different exchanges. If funding rates compress market-wide, all positions experience reduced profitability at the same time, resulting in a global reduction in returns.

Counterparty Clustering

Spreading funds across different platforms or protocols may seem like diversification, but if those platforms share dependencies, the risk remains concentrated.

For example, a trader deposits funds into multiple DeFi lending platforms that all rely on the same stablecoin as collateral. If that stablecoin were to depeg, all lending platforms could become insolvent at once, leading to systemic losses despite the illusion of diversification.

Market Risks

False diversification can also come in the form of systemic market conditions:

- **Exposure to a Single Market Regime:** Many assets and strategies perform well under the same conditions but fail together when conditions change.

- **Interconnected Liquidity Risks:** Traders may assume they have diversified across platforms, but in reality, withdrawals from one can create liquidity crises across others, exacerbating losses.

- **Overlapping Counterparty Risk:** Relying on multiple CEXs or DeFi platforms does not eliminate counterparty risk if they share the same operational dependencies, such as reliance on Tether for settlement liquidity.

How to Achieve True Diversification

To ensure meaningful diversification, traders must take an intentional approach to risk segmentation.

- **Assess Correlation Matrices:** Analyze historical data to identify whether different assets and strategies are genuinely uncorrelated.

- **Diversify Across Distinct Risk Factors:** Instead of focusing on asset count, spread risk across different market inefficiencies, liquidity pools, and trading styles.

- **Segment Counterparty Risk:** Use platforms that do not share dependencies to minimize counterparty concentration.

- **Adapt to Changing Market Environments:** A well-diversified portfolio should remain effective across different volatility regimes and liquidity cycles.

Takeaway

Owning multiple assets or running multiple strategies does not guarantee diversification—true diversification comes from spreading exposure across independent risk factors. Traders must analyze correlations, avoid clustering counterparty risk, and ensure their strategies remain viable in different market environments. Real diversification minimizes systemic exposure, while false diversification only creates a deceptive sense of security.

3. <u>Hedging and Capital Efficiency</u>

Hedging is a fundamental component of risk management that allows traders to minimize unwanted exposure, improving capital efficiency. By using hedging techniques, traders can reduce portfolio volatility and enhance their ability to scale positions without increasing the risk of ruin.

This section examines the role of hedging in delta-neutral strategies, exploring different methods, such as futures hedging, options-based hedging, and cross-asset hedging. It also highlights how effective hedging enables traders to maximize capital deployment while maintaining a controlled risk profile. Understanding these principles is essential for building robust, sustainable trading strategies.

3.1) Why Hedging Is a Game Changer

Hedging is one of the most powerful tools available for managing risk. Unlike speculation, where traders take on exposure hoping to maximize gains, hedging focuses on controlling and mitigating risk while maintaining profit potential. The key principle behind hedging is that reducing return variance tightens performance around EV without lowering overall profitability.

How Hedging Reduces Variance Without Reducing Expected Value

A critical distinction in risk management is that reducing variance does not mean reducing returns. Traders often assume that limiting exposure through hedging results in lower profitability, but in reality, it increases the predictability of returns, which is crucial for long-term compounding.

For example, a trader engaging in funding rate arbitrage shorts a perpetual market to collect the funding rate. Since the trader has no directional edge, the EV of the price-based PNL is zero, assuming the asset has an equal chance of moving up or down. However, the vast majority of the strategy's volatility comes from directional price movements. By hedging the position, therefore removing the directional component of the return, the trader does not reduce the EV of the strategy but significantly decreases the volatility of returns, making the performance more stable and predictable while retaining the same expected profitability.

Lower variance means the trader is far less likely to experience large drawdowns that could wipe out their capital. Even with the same expected return, reducing variance makes returns statistically more reliable over time.

Hedging and Capital Efficiency: A Game Changer

Hedging doesn't just make returns more predictable—it dramatically enhances capital efficiency, allowing traders to scale their exposure safely to generate more returns. Lower volatility means traders can safely scale positions; a strategy that generates stable returns can be leveraged more efficiently than one with high variance.

For example, consider the trader executing funding rate arbitrage by shorting a perpetual market from the previous example:

Without hedging, the trader faces substantial directional price volatility, which limits how much leverage can be safely applied before reaching unacceptable risk levels. However, by hedging the directional volatility, the trader stabilizes the return profile. With a more predictable return stream, the trader can significantly increase leverage, amplifying funding payments received while still maintaining acceptable risk exposure.

By reducing variance, hedging allows traders to optimize risk-adjusted returns, scaling up exposure without increasing downside risk.

Takeaway

Hedging is a game changer because it enhances capital efficiency, reducing variance without reducing expected returns. Traders who hedge effectively can scale their positions with greater confidence, ensuring more predictable performance while minimizing the risk of ruin. By incorporating hedging into delta-neutral strategies, traders can achieve more stable, efficient, and scalable portfolio management.

3.2) Hedging Techniques

Hedging is a core risk management tool that allows traders to reduce downside exposure while maintaining profitability. However, not all hedging methods are created equal. Choosing the right hedge depends on the trader's strategy, risk tolerance, and market conditions. The goal of hedging is not only to eliminate risk, but also to optimize risk-adjusted returns and capital efficiency.

Before implementing a hedge, traders must consider three key factors:

- **Impact on Profitability:** Does the hedge significantly reduce expected returns?

- **Cost and Liquidity:** Are there funding costs, option premiums, or execution slippage to account for?

- **Unintended Risks:** Does the hedge introduce new exposures, such as correlation risk or counterparty risk?

Futures-Based Hedging

Traders use short futures or perpetual contracts to offset long exposure, effectively reducing directional risk while maintaining capital efficiency. A key advantage of using futures for hedging is that they have a fixed delta of -1 when shorting, meaning their sensitivity to price movements remains constant. As a result, they do not require frequent rebalancing, unlike options or other hedging instruments with gamma exposure. However, a key challenge is that funding rates can fluctuate, sometimes turning negative, making the hedge costly over time.

Options-Based Hedging

Options provide asymmetric risk protection, allowing traders to hedge against large price swings while keeping upside potential. This method is best for protecting against tail risk and sudden volatility spikes. A trader might buy protective put options to limit downside risk without needing to exit a spot position. However, option premiums can be expensive, which can reduce cost efficiency if not carefully managed.

Cross-Asset Hedging: Leveraging Correlated Markets

Instead of directly hedging an asset, traders can use correlated assets to offset exposure, reducing hedge costs while maintaining exposure to market inefficiencies. For example, a participant holding ETH for on-chain yield strategies may hedge their exposure by shorting LDO, which has a higher funding rate than ETH (therefore will pay more), assuming a high correlation between the two assets. By doing so, they can maximize funding revenue while maintaining yield generation. However, correlations are not static and can break down unexpectedly, leading to imperfect hedging.

Structural Hedging Through On-Chain Borrowing and Yield Strategies

On-chain money markets can be used to recreate short positions. This approach is particularly useful for hedging assets that do not have derivatives available, such as stablecoins. For example, a trader borrows and sells a stablecoin against BTC collateral. By effectively shorting a stablecoin used as collateral in another position, the participant eliminates counterparty risk associated with the stablecoin. However, risks such as liquidation and smart contract vulnerabilities must be carefully managed.

The Trade-Offs and Key Considerations for Different Hedging Approaches

Each hedging method comes with its own advantages and challenges. Futures and perpetuals offer a simple and cost-efficient way to hedge but can be affected by unpredictable funding rates. Options are ideal for tail-risk protection while keeping upside potential, but high premiums can reduce efficiency and fluctuating delta can complicate management. Cross-asset hedging is flexible and often cheaper, but it carries the risk of correlation breakdowns. On-chain borrowing provides asset diversity, but it comes with liquidation and smart contract risks.

When selecting the right hedge, traders should consider liquidity and execution risks, as some hedging tools work best in liquid markets, while others may suffer from slippage. Additionally, hedging costs versus benefits must be carefully analyzed, including funding fees, premiums, and interest rates, to ensure profitability. The most effective hedge is one that neutralizes risk while keeping returns stable and cost-efficient.

Takeaway

Hedging is not just about eliminating risk—it is about optimizing capital efficiency and preserving returns. Different hedging methods serve different purposes, and traders must select the right tool based on their market exposure and risk tolerance. The best hedges minimize risk without unnecessarily reducing profitability, ensuring traders can scale positions safely while maintaining predictable performance.

4. <u>Key Principles of Delta-Neutral Strategies</u>

Delta-neutral strategies are designed to extract value from market inefficiencies while maintaining minimal directional risk. However, the long-term success of these strategies depends on continuous adaptation, risk control, and the ability to identify sustainable inefficiencies. Effective execution requires not only technical knowledge but also a disciplined approach to monitoring, adjusting, and refining trading positions.

This section explores the key principles behind optimizing delta-neutral strategies, including market inefficiency identification, adaptive risk management, and capital deployment techniques. By mastering these concepts, traders can build resilient, scalable strategies that generate consistent returns under varying market conditions.

4.1) The Core Mechanisms of Delta-Neutral Strategies

Delta-neutral strategies are designed to minimize market exposure while extracting returns from structural inefficiencies. By reducing variance through the elimination of directional exposure, delta-neutral strategies create more stable and predictable returns, enabling traders to scale their positions and capture inefficiencies with higher confidence and extreme capital efficiency.

What Is Delta?

Delta measures how much the price of a position changes in response to movements in the underlying asset. It is a core concept in derivatives pricing and risk management.

- Delta values range from -1 to +1:
    - A long position has a positive delta—if the asset price increases, the position gains value.

- A short position has a negative delta—if the asset price decreases, the position gains value.

- Options and Delta Sensitivity:

  - **Fixed Delta:** A futures contract has a fixed delta of +1 (long) or -1 (short), meaning its price moves in lockstep with the underlying asset.

  - **Fluctuating Delta:** An option's delta changes as the underlying price fluctuates, requiring adjustments to maintain delta neutrality.

- Beta-Adjusted Delta for Cross-Asset Hedging:

  - In cross-asset hedging, traders use beta-adjusted delta to account for differences in volatility and correlation between assets.

  - **Example:** If BTC and ETH have a strong correlation but ETH has higher volatility, a trader shorting ETH to hedge BTC exposure must adjust their position size based on ETH's beta relative to BTC to achieve delta neutrality.

Why Does Delta Matter?

Understanding delta is crucial for managing risk, as it determines how much directional exposure a position has and helps traders effectively hedge price movements. By knowing the delta of a position, traders can take steps to neutralize price risk while still capitalizing on market inefficiencies.

For example, a trader holding a long BTC spot position has a +1 delta, meaning if BTC increases by $1,000, the trader gains $1,000. Conversely, shorting 1 BTC perpetual contract with a -1 delta offsets this exposure, creating a delta-neutral position where price changes no longer impact overall profitability.

Offsetting Long and Short Positions

Traders hold equal long and short positions to neutralize price risk.

For example, a trader long BTC in the spot market shorts an equivalent amount of BTC perpetual contracts to create a delta-neutral position.

Options-Based Delta Hedging

Traders adjust exposure dynamically using options to maintain delta neutrality.

For example, a trader long ETH buys ETH put options to hedge against downside moves, adjusting delta based on market conditions.

Cross-Asset Hedging for Delta Neutrality

Instead of direct hedging, traders use correlated assets to minimize exposure.

For example, a trader with BTC exposure shorts ETH perpetuals, benefiting from their strong correlation while increasing funding payments received. By beta-adjusting the hedge size, the trader ensures the ETH short effectively neutralizes BTC exposure.

Takeaway

Delta is a measure of how much the price of a position changes in response to movements in the underlying asset. Understanding delta allows traders to structure positions that minimize market exposure while extracting returns from inefficiencies. By effectively managing delta, traders can construct delta-neutral positions that remain insulated from price fluctuations, ensuring stable and predictable returns.

4.2) Identifying and Exploiting Market Inefficiencies

Market inefficiencies arise when prices, rates, or volatility deviate from their fair value, often due to market structure limitations. These inefficiencies create profit opportunities for traders who can systematically exploit them using delta-neutral strategies.

Common causes of inefficiencies include:

- Lack of liquidity – Thinly traded markets can cause price distortions and mispricings.

- Liquidity fragmentation – Differences across trading venues create arbitrage opportunities.

- Structural or regulatory constraints – Market access limitations or trading restrictions prevent efficient price discovery.

- Lagging and reactionary mechanisms – Delayed execution, data updates, or slow market responses allow inefficiencies to persist longer than they should.

Price Misalignment

Price misalignment occurs when the same asset trades at different prices across exchanges due to liquidity fragmentation or execution delays. This creates arbitrage opportunities where traders can buy the asset where it is cheaper and sell it where it is more expensive while maintaining a delta-neutral position. Price misalignments are common in fragmented and less liquid markets, where trading activity varies significantly between platforms.

For example, a trader notices that ETH is trading at $3,000 on Exchange A and $3,050 on Exchange B. By simultaneously buying ETH on Exchange A and selling it on Exchange B, the trader locks in a $50 risk-free profit per unit traded, which he will realize when the price converges and he closes the trade. It is important to account for fees and slippage to ensure profitability.

Rate Misalignment

Rate misalignment happens when lending, borrowing, staking, or other rates differ across platforms due to liquidity imbalances and variations in supply and demand. Traders can exploit this inefficiency by borrowing at a lower rate on one platform and lending at a higher rate on another, all while hedging directional exposure. Such inefficiencies persist when liquidity is unevenly distributed between CeFi and DeFi lending markets or when platform-specific incentives distort rates. An important factor covered in depth later is that certain stablecoins are based on reactionary mechanisms, which always lag behind others in adjusting rates, creating arbitrage opportunities for traders who can detect these discrepancies.

For example, a trader borrows Stablecoin A at an annualized interest rate of 8% and then trades it for Stablecoin B, which offers a 12% yield for staking, capturing a 4% spread.

Funding rates in perpetual futures markets also fall into this category. In an efficient market with unlimited capital and no restrictions, funding rates would remain close to the risk-free rate. However, in reality, funding rates can remain substantially higher than the risk-free rate while the risk of collecting them remains low. This misalignment creates an opportunity where traders can enter delta-neutral positions to collect positive funding payments while hedging price risk.

For example, a trader notices that BTC perpetual contracts on Exchange A offer a +0.1% hourly funding rate. The trader shorts the BTC perpetual contract while simultaneously holding an equivalent amount of spot BTC. As a result, the trader collects the funding rate payments while maintaining a delta-neutral position.

Volatility Mispricing

Volatility mispricing is an inefficiency that arises when implied volatility in derivatives markets deviates from realized volatility or fair market expectations. This creates opportunities for traders to enter volatility-based arbitrage trades.

For example, a trader identifies that ETH options are priced with an implied volatility of 80%, but believes it should only be 20%. The trader sells the overpriced options while hedging directional exposure through other option spreads or futures, profiting from the eventual reversion of volatility pricing.

However, this type of inefficiency approaches options trading, which is outside the scope of this book and will not be covered in depth.

Evaluating the Sustainability of an Inefficiency

- **Liquidity Constraints:** Can the inefficiency be arbitraged at scale?

- **Market Structure Risks:** Is the inefficiency likely to persist, or will it correct quickly due to increased competition?

- **Execution Costs:** Are transaction fees, slippage, and funding rates low enough to make arbitrage profitable?

- **Regulatory Factors:** Could legal restrictions limit access to specific arbitrage opportunities?

The sustainability of an inefficiency depends on its persistence before market forces correct it. Inefficiencies that are easily arbitraged tend to disappear quickly as more traders exploit them, making them less viable over time. The ability to scale an inefficiency without significantly impacting market prices is crucial, as high participation can diminish returns.

Takeaway

Market inefficiencies provide lucrative opportunities for delta-neutral traders, allowing them to profit from pricing, rates, and volatility discrepancies without taking on directional risk. Understanding the underlying causes of inefficiencies—such as liquidity fragmentation, lagging mechanisms, and regulatory constraints—helps traders predict and assess these inefficiencies. Identifying and exploiting inefficiencies requires careful execution, cost assessment, and continuous monitoring to ensure long-term profitability.

4.3) Applying Risk Management in Delta-Neutral Strategies

Effective risk management ensures that traders maintain consistent returns while avoiding unexpected losses. Without proper controls, even well-structured delta-neutral trades can become highly vulnerable to unforeseen disruptions.

Position Sizing and Leverage Control

Proper position sizing is crucial to ensure that capital allocation is balanced and risk exposure is controlled. Positions that are too large expose the strategy to all known risks, including liquidation due to volatility, counterparty risk from concentration, and execution risks. Even delta-neutral strategies can become high-risk if positions are too large relative to available capital.

For example, a trader engaged in funding rate arbitrage may use excessive leverage. If violent price movement causes margin requirements to increase, even if their position remains delta-neutral, the trader could face liquidation before he has time to rebalance his positions. Maintaining conservative leverage and appropriately sizing positions ensures capital resilience in volatile conditions.

Stop-Loss and Liquidation Protection

Risk needs to be capped to prevent catastrophic losses from rare market events. Delta-neutral traders must incorporate stop-loss mechanisms that account for margin and liquidation risks, rather than relying solely on price-based triggers.

For example, a trader holding a cross-exchange arbitrage position sets stop-losses not on the price of the asset but on the margin level relative to total capital. This ensures that if the price becomes too volatile, both sides of the position are closed, preventing the trader from being left with unwanted exposure.

Real-Time Monitoring and Adjustments

Delta-neutral strategies require continuous oversight to ensure that neutrality is maintained. Markets shift, funding rates change, and correlation structures can evolve, requiring adjustments to remain risk-controlled.

For example, a trader exploiting a rate misalignment between lending and borrowing markets must regularly rebalance positions to ensure that the spread remains profitable. If lending rates drop significantly, the position may no longer justify the capital allocation, requiring either an adjustment or closure.

Counterparty and Execution Risk Mitigation

Exchange failures, smart contract risks, and counterparty insolvencies pose a threat to delta-neutral traders. Spreading capital across multiple counterparties reduces concentration risk.

For example, a trader deploying capital into DeFi lending platforms ensures risk diversification by using multiple lending pools rather than a single venue. Similarly, in CeFi, funds are distributed across multiple exchanges to hedge against withdrawal freezes or insolvencies.

Adapting to Market Conditions and Stress Testing

Market conditions evolve, and assumptions about correlations, liquidity, and funding conditions may break down. Traders must be proactive in recognizing when inefficiencies start to normalize or when risks begin to outweigh potential rewards.

Additionally, traders should simulate extreme market conditions—such as liquidity crises, funding rate collapses, or volatility spikes—to assess the robustness of their delta-neutral approaches. By using stress testing strategies, traders can identify weak points and preemptively adjust risk parameters to avoid significant drawdowns.

Takeaway

Delta-neutral strategies require robust risk management to ensure consistent returns and capital preservation. Position sizing, stop-loss mechanisms, real-time monitoring, and stress testing are essential tools for mitigating these risks. Successful delta-neutral traders focus on adaptability, disciplined execution, and resilience against evolving market conditions to ensure long-term sustainability.

Chapter 4: Core Strategies

This chapter focuses on the core delta-neutral strategies that enable traders to generate consistent returns without exposing themselves to directional market risks. These strategies are more than isolated tactics; they are essential tools for constructing a diversified and resilient market approach. By executing different types of strategies, traders can diversify risk, enhance their risk-reward profile, and adapt to changing market conditions. The ability to capture various types of inefficiencies provides flexibility—either by being more selective on entry conditions for higher returns or by deploying strategies at scale to generate returns on larger amounts of capital.

Throughout this chapter, we will explore key strategies, including arbitrage strategies, lending strategies, liquidity provision, staking, and CPVs. We will also address how incentives and on-chain yield-trading can be integrated into an overall strategy. Each section will dive into the mechanics, practical applications, and real-world considerations of these strategies, equipping you with the knowledge to execute them effectively and integrate them into a cohesive trading framework.

1. Arbitrage Strategies

Arbitrage strategies are foundational delta-neutral strategies. They exploit misalignments in price, rates, and volatility across markets, allowing traders to generate predictable returns. The dynamic nature of cryptocurrency markets—characterized by fragmented liquidity, volatile funding rates, and structural differences across venues—creates a fertile environment for such strategies.

The following subsections will break down key arbitrage strategies, from spot arbitrage to cross-venue perpetual arbitrage. Each strategy will be explained with practical examples, advanced concepts, and common pitfalls to avoid.

1.1) Spot-to-Spot Arbitrage

Spot arbitrage is a straightforward delta-neutral strategy but requires careful execution to be profitable. It involves exploiting price discrepancies for the same asset across two spot markets. These inefficiencies often arise due to liquidity fragmentation or periods of high volatility, such as token launches or major news events. Additionally, inefficiencies can result from dynamics that restrict the free movement of capital. The most important process in spot arbitrage is understanding the factors that create inefficiencies, which is crucial for detecting such opportunities and effectively taking advantage of them.

Strategy Mechanics

At its core, spot arbitrage involves the following steps:

i. Identify a price discrepancy for an asset between two platforms (e.g., a CEX and a DEX).

ii. Buy the asset on the lower-priced platform.

iii. Transfer the asset to the higher-priced platform.

iv. Sell the asset at a premium to lock in a profit.

v. Repeat until the price discrepancy no longer covers fees.

vi. In cases where the asset cannot be quickly resold, it is important to hedge exposure.

Simplified Example

Consider ETH that is trading at $1,900 on Uniswap and $2,000 on Binance:

- Buy ETH on Uniswap at $1,900.

- Transfer ETH to Binance.

- Sell ETH on Binance at $2,000, netting a $100 profit per ETH before fees.

This process continues until arbitrage closes the price gap. It's worth noting that for this strategy to be truly delta-neutral, the exposure to the asset during the transfer should ideally be hedged with a perpetual futures contract. However, this is rarely feasible for less liquid tokens due to limited derivatives markets, which is also why such inefficiencies are much more likely to present themselves for these smaller tokens.

Pitfalls and Mistakes to Avoid

Understanding how losses occur is critical to avoiding them. Spot arbitrage has inherent risks that can result in losses if not carefully managed.

- **Misjudging Fees:** Misjudging fees including AMM fees, gas fees, and CEX trading, deposit, and withdrawal fees, all of which can erode profits. Accurate fee estimation is crucial for success.

- **Misjudging Spread and Slippage:** Thin order books or liquidity pools can lead to slippage, reducing profitability. Considering spreads and ensuring sufficient market liquidity are both critical steps before executing trades.

- **Getting Trapped with Unwanted Exposure:** Delays from exchange deposits and blockchain confirmation times can impact execution. This is significant because if the token exposure is not covered with a derivative, the trader has directional exposure to the token until the deposit is completed and they sell.

- **Ignoring Counterparty Risk:** Using unreliable exchanges, which may be less efficient and present more arbitrage opportunities, may also lead to trapped funds.

Case Study: The Kimchi Premium

One of the most well-known examples of spot arbitrage is the kimchi premium. This phenomenon refers to the persistent price discrepancies for Bitcoin and other cryptocurrencies on South Korean exchanges compared to global markets. Traders are able to buy Bitcoin on international platforms and sell it at significantly higher prices on South Korean exchanges, generating substantial profits. Notably, this was how Alameda Research, the trading firm founded by Sam Bankman-Fried, made its first significant profits, leveraging these discrepancies to scale its operations.

In 2025, South Korean exchanges still enforce strict regulations that prevent foreigners from easily opening accounts. This regulatory landscape continues to create unique dynamics where highly anticipated airdrops or newly listed tokens often sell for significantly higher prices on South Korean exchanges. This is driven by strong local demand, as Korean buyers seek exposure, while the restricted market access limits the number of sellers able to capitalize on these price discrepancies.

1.2) Spot-to-Perpetual Arbitrage

Spot-to-perpetual arbitrage, also known as a basis trade, is a staple delta-neutral strategy that exploits price differences between spot markets and perpetual futures contracts. Traders take advantage of these inefficiencies by setting up a delta-neutral position:

- Buying the asset in the spot market while simultaneously shorting the same asset in the perpetual futures market.

- The price difference (or basis) between the two markets allows traders to lock in profits when contango (perps priced higher than spot) disappears.

- This strategy naturally captures both funding rate payments and basis spread profits, since funding rates rise when basis widens.

Crypto Majors Naturally Exhibit a Positive Basis

Crypto majors like BTC and ETH consistently trade in contango, meaning perpetual futures prices tend to be higher than spot prices due to structural market imbalances. From mid-2020 to mid-2023, ETH's median funding rate was +6–7% annually on an open interest-weighted basis, even taking into account the 2022 bear market data. This persistent positive funding rate reflects the imbalance between leverage demand and supply—many traders are inherently long and seek to take advantage of future fiat inflows with leverage beyond their existing capital.

Further reinforcing this trend, most liquid derivatives venues have a positive baseline funding, meaning that when spot and perpetual prices are in line and the basis is negligible, the funding rate will snap to a positive value instead of 0, which would be more intuitive.

Execution Process

Executing a spot-to-perpetual arbitrage trade requires precise timing and capital efficiency. The basis spread must be wide enough to cover fees in case the funding rate doesn't persist, and the amount of leverage must balance between capital efficiency and preventing liquidation.

  i. **Identify the Basis Spread:** Look for a significant divergence between spot and perpetual futures prices. Monitoring funding rates can help detect assets that present an opportunity.

  ii. **Buy the Asset in the Spot Market:** Acquire the asset at the lower spot price.

  iii. **Short an Equivalent Amount in Perpetual Futures:** Open a short position on the perpetual contract trading in contango to hedge price exposure.

  iv. **Collect Funding Rate Payments until Basis Disappears:** The trader will receive funding rate payments until the basis disappears, at which point he can exit the position to capture the basis spread and avoid unfavorable funding rates.

Practical Example: Capturing the Basis Spread

The participant exploits a positive basis on ETH:

- ETH spot price: $3,000.

- ETH perpetual futures price: $3,150 (5% contango).

- The trader buys ETH in the spot market and shorts ETH perps, locking in a $150 per ETH basis spread when prices converge.

- As long as ETH perps trade at a contango, the trader will receive funding payments for being short.

- When prices converge, the trader will stop receiving funding payments and will be able to close to position to lock in profits from the basis spread captured.

To enhance returns, participants can leverage yield-generating collateral; instead of holding spot ETH directly, the trader can use ETH LSDs like stETH, which generate staking rewards while maintaining exposure to the underlying asset. This setup allows the trader to compound returns by capturing both staking yield and funding payments.

Common Pitfalls and Risk Management Techniques

- **Excessive Leverage:** While leverage allows traders to boost capital efficiency and increase returns, overleveraging increases the risk of forced liquidations, even in a delta-neutral trade. If the price is volatile and the participant fails to rebalance positions, one side of the delta-neutral position may be liquidated, leading to fees and unwanted directional exposure.

- **Lack of Liquidity:** For smaller markets, a lack of liquidity could prevent the position from being efficiently closed, forcing the trader to either remain stuck in the position while funding potentially turns unfavorable or suffer high slippage when exiting. It is crucial to select markets that can support sufficient position sizes.

- **Frequent Exposure Rebalance:** An exchange may become insolvent, leading to the loss of funds held on the platform. To counteract this, it is a good idea to spread funds between multiple exchanges. If one exchange has a significant positive PNL, it can be a good idea to close and reopen the trade to realize profits and move them off the exchange (rebalancing counterparty exposure).

- **Fees Projection:** Trading fees, withdrawal/deposit fees, and the probable duration of the trade (to estimate funding payments) must be accounted for in profitability calculations.

Case Study: The Ethena Basis Trade

Ethena's USDe is seen and used as a stablecoin, but in reality, it is a tokenized basis trade on ETH. The position is structured as follows:

- Ethena holds ETH LSTs (e.g., stETH or rETH) to earn staking rewards while maintaining the underlying ETH exposure.

- Simultaneously, Ethena shorts ETH perpetual futures to neutralize price exposure and capture consistently positive funding rates.

This method provides dual yields from staking rewards and funding rate collection, maximizing capital efficiency. Additionally, Ethena addresses each risk vector effectively to optimize the risk profile of the strategy:

- **Liquidation Risk:** Ethena uses little to no leverage, minimizing the risk of liquidation during market volatility. Additionally, advanced monitoring systems ensure real-time adjustments to maintain stability.

- **Liquidity Risk:** Ethena operates exclusively on ETH and BTC markets, the two most liquid crypto assets, reducing the risk of being unable to enter or exit positions efficiently.

- **Custodial Risk:** Ethena employs an off-exchange settlement solution that allows them to keep their margin with a separate custodian, mitigating exposure to exchange insolvency.

- **Execution Risk:** Since basis trades are long-duration strategies, trading fees are less significant compared to the cumulative funding payments collected over time.

Ethena's carry trade has proven to be an effective delta-neutral strategy, consistently generating profits through high funding rates and persistent contango. The ability to use liquid staked ETH (LSTs) as collateral enhances capital efficiency, while robust risk management provides a scalable and low-effort strategy (for holders) with an attractive risk profile, which has led to its widespread adoption.

Takeaways

Spot-to-perpetual arbitrage is one of the most effective ways to profit from market inefficiencies in crypto derivatives. By understanding execution mechanics, market structure, and risk factors, traders can consistently generate low-risk, delta-neutral returns while benefiting from both funding payments and basis spreads.

1.3) Perpetual-to-Perpetual Arbitrage

Perpetual-to-perpetual arbitrage aims to exploit price and/or funding rate discrepancies between perpetual contracts across different trading venues. These discrepancies may arise from structural differences in trading contracts, variations in funding mechanisms between venues, or dynamics that restrain the free flow of capital. By capturing the basis and/or net funding payments resulting from these discrepancies, traders can achieve predictable returns without taking directional market risks.

Precision and Risk in Cross-Perpetual Arbitrage

It is important to note that cross-perpetual arbitrage requires more precise analysis than spot-to-perpetual arbitrage and should not be executed based on the simple detection of a discrepancy, as most will likely disappear before the funding payments cover fees. Instead, traders need a strong structural rationale to ensure the discrepancy will persist long enough to realize profitability.

Compared to a basis trade, cross-perpetual arbitrage has a higher risk of becoming unprofitable since funding rates don't need to flip against the trader; the discrepancy between venues only needs to close/reverse. However, when successful, this strategy can offer significantly higher returns due to the availability of leverage for both sides of the trade.

For example, while it can be optimized by using some leverage on the perpetual leg of the position and holding a yield-generating asset for the spot position, a 20% funding rate will yield approximately 20% APY for a basis trade. In contrast, a 20% funding discrepancy between perpetual swaps can be highly leveraged (e.g., 5x leverage generating 100% APY for the duration of the trade).

Strategy Mechanics

The execution of cross-perpetual arbitrage involves the following steps:

i. Identify a funding rate disparity for the same asset between two trading venues.

ii. Open a long position on the venue with the lower funding rate.

iii. Open a short position on the venue with the higher funding rate.

iv. Collect the net funding payment from the rate differential until the discrepancy normalizes.

For example, consider two ETH perpetual contracts:

i. Venue A has a negative funding rate of -0.01% (traders are paid to hold long positions).

ii. Venue B has a positive funding rate of +0.03% (traders pay to hold long positions).

iii. Open a long ETH position on Venue A and a short ETH position on Venue B.

iv. The trader collects the net funding payment of 0.04% for the duration of the trade.

This strategy is profitable as long as the funding rate differential exceeds the fees incurred when opening, maintaining, and closing the positions. Even if both funding rates are positive or both are negative—meaning one position pays funding fees—the strategy remains viable as long as the funding fees paid are less than the funding fees received from the other position.

Common Pitfalls and Risk Management Techniques

Perpetual-to-perpetual arbitrage shares many considerations with a basis trade. It is crucial to understand how loss may occur to avoid these situations.

- **Excessive Leverage:** Overleveraging increases the risk of forced liquidations, even in a delta-neutral trade. If the price is volatile and the participant fails to rebalance positions, one side of the delta-neutral position may be liquidated, leading to fees and unwanted directional exposure.

- **Liquidity Risk:** For smaller markets, a lack of liquidity could prevent the position from being efficiently closed, forcing the trader to either remain stuck in the position while funding potentially turns unfavorable or suffer high slippage when exiting.

- **Custodial Risk:** An exchange may become insolvent, leading to the loss of funds held on the platform. To counteract this, it is a good idea to spread funds between multiple exchanges. If one exchange has significant positive PNL, it can be a good idea to close and reopen the trade to realize profits and move them off the exchange (rebalancing counterparty exposure).

- **Execution and Fee Considerations:** Trading fees, withdrawal/deposit fees, and the probable duration of the trade (to estimate funding payments) must be accounted for in profitability calculations.

- **Funding Rate Convergence:** As opposed to a basis trade, perpetual-to-perpetual arbitrage will not always capture a basis and will aim to capitalize on funding rate discrepancies between venues caused by structural differences in funding mechanisms. This introduces the risk that the discrepancy disappears before funding payments have covered fees paid for entering and exiting the position. It is crucial to take a calculated bet with a robust thesis for why the funding rate discrepancy should persist long enough to achieve profitability.

Case Study: BNB Perpetual Markets on Binance and Hyperliquid

At the time of writing, Hyperliquid tends to have higher funding rates because of structural reasons, such as some actors running funding rate arbitrage relying on custodian services that do not yet support Hyperliquid. As a result, funding arbitrage on Hyperliquid is less efficient, creating opportunities for persistent funding rate discrepancies.

In addition, while the baseline funding for both Binance and Hyperliquid is 0.01% per eight hours, Binance makes an exception for its own token, BNB. On Binance, BNB has a baseline funding rate of 0%, compared to 0.01% per eight hours on Hyperliquid.

This structural difference in funding mechanisms further amplifies the funding differential between Binance and Hyperliquid for the BNB token. Hyperliquid tends to have higher funding rates than Binance due to liquidity dynamics, and BNB's funding rates on Binance tend to be lower than on other venues due to specific funding rate mechanisms; this creates an opportunity.

If a trader were to exploit this inefficiency, he would follow these actions:

- On Binance, open a long BNB perpetual futures position with a baseline funding rate of 0%, using 5x leverage.

- On Hyperliquid, open a short BNB perpetual futures position with an hourly baseline funding rate of 0.00125% (0.01%/8), using 5x leverage.

- The trader aims to collect, on average, 0.00625% (0.00125%*5) in net funding payments per hour, which is equivalent to more than 50% APY.

This case study demonstrates an inefficiency caused by differences in funding mechanisms and the inefficient movement of capital between markets. Such structural factors create persistent opportunities for traders to capitalize on funding rate discrepancies, highlighting the importance of understanding the underlying causes of these inefficiencies for successful strategy execution.

2. **Lending Strategies**

Money markets play a vital role in enabling delta-neutral strategies on-chain. These markets provide three essential components: access to leverage, the capacity to hedge, and yields through lending. Each of these elements contributes to building efficient, risk-managed portfolios in DeFi.

Every money market transaction involves a simple exchange: lenders earn interest by providing liquidity, enabling leverage, while borrowers pay interest to use this leverage for strategies like hedging or yield farming. This dynamic forms the foundation of money markets, aligning capital providers with those seeking efficient deployment.

Money markets thus act as the backbone for capital efficiency and risk management in DeFi. This section explores how leverage, hedging, and lending opportunities can be utilized effectively, beginning with the mechanics and risks of leveraging through looping.

2.1) Leverage

The creation of leverage via money markets is achieved through a method known as looping or folding. This technique involves a cyclical process of supplying collateral, borrowing another asset against it, and selling the borrowed asset into additional collateral to supply. Through this repetitive mechanism, participants can achieve significant leverage ratios.

The Process of Looping

The looping process consists of four key actions:

> i. Supplying an asset as collateral.
>
> ii. Borrowing against the collateral.
>
> iii. Swapping the borrowed assets back to the collateral asset.
>
> iv. Supplying the swapped assets as additional collateral.

This cycle can be repeated multiple times to achieve the desired leverage level. The maximum leverage attainable is governed by the LLTV ratio imposed by the market, calculated as:

Maximum Leverage = 1 / (1 - LLTV)

The number of loops required to reach a target leverage can be determined using the formula:

$$Number\ of\ Loops = ln(1 - LLTV) / ln(targetLTV) - 1$$

Note that loops are often performed by lending and borrowing correlated assets, such as two stablecoins or an asset and its derivative (e.g., wETH and wstETH). This approach protects the position from liquidation with the correlated price movements of the assets, ensuring the LTV ratio remains relatively stable.

Calculating Position Yield

The yield of a leveraged position is determined by the difference between the returns generated by the collateral and the cost of borrowing. The formula for position yield is:

$$Position\ Yield = (Leverage \times Collateral\ Yield) - ((Leverage - 1) \times Borrow\ Cost)$$

Understanding this formula is crucial for assessing whether the looping strategy will remain profitable over time.

One-Click Looping

Platforms exist to facilitate looping. Protocols such as Dolomite and Contango offer one-click maximum leverage features, streamlining the leveraging process. These platforms achieve this functionality through the use of *flash loans*, enabling seamless and efficient execution.

Flash loans are a type of uncollateralized loan in DeFi that allows users to borrow assets instantly and repay them within the same transaction. If the loan is not repaid by the end of the transaction, the entire operation is reversed.

Leveraging flash loans, Dolomite's system allows users to maximize their leverage efficiently, minimizing manual interactions. Positions can also be unlooped in one click, enhancing flexibility and simplifying the exit process.

Analyzing Dynamic Interest Rates

Fluctuating borrow rates can lead to situations where the cost of borrowing exceeds the yield generated by the collateral, rendering the position unprofitable. Since entering and exiting a position incurs fees, exiting as soon as it becomes unprofitable may result in a loss if the accrued yield has not covered the fees.

Before entering a position, it is essential to evaluate the yield relative to the fees incurred and the potential rise in borrowing costs associated with utilization rates. Understanding the IRM used by the market is critical for determining the maximum borrowing interest rate and identifying the utilization rate at which borrowing costs begin to rise sharply.

This assessment ensures a clear understanding of the break-even point before committing to the position.

Analyzing Oracle Dependency

Oracles are the data source for the price of an asset. These feeds are essential for protocols, especially borrowing and lending platforms, which rely on external price feeds for tasks like calculating liquidations. They determine asset prices on money markets, which in turn dictate LTV ratios and decide whether a position will be liquidated.

Many looping strategies rely on correlated assets, such as lending weETH and borrowing wstETH. Theoretically, the correlation between these assets should prevent liquidation since their prices move in harmony. However, depending on the oracle used, an inaccuracy or depeg caused by factors like a large holder selling or a market event creating a downward price wick on the collateral asset can trigger liquidation. Similarly, a sudden spike in the borrowed asset's price can lead to forced liquidations.

There are two primary types of oracles: market rate oracles and exchange rate oracles.

- **Market Rate Oracles:** These oracles aggregate prices from multiple sources, such as on-chain DEXs and CEXs. For instance, a Redstone ETH oracle uses twenty-one different price feeds to create a composite index price. Market rate oracles are sensitive to depegs because they directly reflect real-time market pressures. For example, a 5% depeg of weETH during a black swan event could result in the liquidation of a leveraged position on weETH/wstETH, even if the assets are fundamentally correlated.

- **Exchange Rate Oracles:** Also known as NAV or fundamental oracles, these oracles determine an asset's price based on its underlying value rather than market fluctuations. These are commonly used for assets like LSDs and LRTs, which are backed by staked or restaked ETH. Such oracles are less sensitive to market depegs, providing greater protection to borrowers.

Most money markets clearly display the type of oracle being used on their front ends, and in cases where they don't, users can verify the oracle via the protocol's on-chain contracts. As a general rule, market rate oracles are more secure for protocols, while exchange rate oracles benefit borrowers.

Case Study: Looping Opportunity on Morpho

An opportunity for looping yields arose when the OETH market went live on Morpho Labs with the following settings:

- **Loan-to-Liquidation Value (LLTV):** 91.5%, allowing participants to achieve up to 11.75x leverage.

- **Oracle Type:** The protocol utilized a fundamental exchange rate oracle.

- **Interest Rate Model (IRM):** Capped at a borrow rate of 2.84% for 100% utilization.

- **OETH Collateral Yield:** The OETH market offered a yield of 15.06%.

- **Yield Calculation:** With a collateral yield of 15.06%, the effective position APR was calculated as:

  (0.1506 × 11.5) - (0.0284 × 10.75) = 142.66% APR

This opportunity was exceptional because it combined high looped yields with minimized risks. The depeg risk was effectively mitigated by the use of an exchange rate oracle, which values assets based on their underlying fundamentals rather than market fluctuations, and the risk of dynamic borrowing rates was eliminated by the capped borrow rate of 2.84%, ensuring predictable borrowing costs.

The remaining risks were limited to the uncontrollable exploit risks of both the Morpho platform and the OETH collateral. While these risks cannot be entirely eliminated, they are less likely to occur compared to the more common risks of depegging or borrowing rate volatility, making the risk-reward/EV of this position extremely favorable.

Note that speed is required to capitalize on such opportunities, as available liquidity was quickly depleted.

2.2) Hedging

Money markets play a critical role in enabling hedging strategies within DeFi. Hedging through money markets provides unique advantages, particularly for assets that cannot be effectively hedged using derivatives or that are not accepted as collateral for derivatives margin. This subsection explores the purpose, process, and practical implementation of hedging via money markets.

Purpose of Hedging via Money Markets

i. **Hedging Assets Without Available Derivatives:** For some assets, derivatives products enabling shorts are unavailable. Money markets fill this gap by allowing users to borrow and sell these assets, creating a hedge against exposure.

ii. **Using All Assets as Collateral for Hedging:** Most platforms that offer linear perpetual contracts, often referred to as stablecoin contracts, are settled in USDC/USDT. Money markets allow participants to use volatile assets (and otherwise unsupported stablecoins) as collateral to create a hedge, offering broader flexibility for risk management.

Hedging Process Review

Hedging via money markets involves borrowing and selling the asset that the participant seeks to offset the exposure of. The following steps outline the general process:

i. **Provide Collateral:** Supply a correlated asset as collateral to improve the stability of the position's LTV.

ii. **Borrow and Sell the Asset to Hedge:** This is the action that offsets exposure to the asset.

iii. **Loop the Hedge (Optional):** Supply more collateral with the proceeds from the sale of the borrowed asset, borrow more, and repeat to create a looped hedge.

Borrowing and selling an asset creates a hedge by establishing an obligation to repurchase it later. If the asset's price declines, the cost to repurchase decreases, resulting in a profit. For instance, when borrowing 1 ETH and selling it at $4,000, if the price drops to $2,000, then repurchasing it costs $2,000, yielding a $2,000 profit. This is essentially what happens behind the scenes for a short position.

Risks in Hedging

Hedging via money markets involves inherent risks of utilizing money markets and leverage:

- **Exploit Risk:** Depositing collateral and borrowing assets on money markets exposes participants to the unavoidable risk of exploits. These vulnerabilities are tied to smart contracts and security practices of the platform.

- **Liquidation Risk:** Price volatility or asset depegging can result in liquidation. Even with correlated assets or stablecoins, sudden market shifts or external pressures can lead to an LTV exceeding safe thresholds, triggering forced liquidations.

Case Study: Hedging ETH Liquid Restaked Tokens

In 2024, a common strategy involved holding and looping ETH LRTs to accumulate points from restaking protocols. These points translated into airdrops, providing an additional yield.

To hedge directional exposure to ETH price, participants could short ETH perpetuals. However, this approach carried a key risk: exposure to the tail risks of the specific ETH LRT. If the derivative associated with the LRT were exploited, the ETH price would remain unaffected, leaving the short position ineffective as a hedge.

Money markets offered a solution by allowing participants to hedge the specific ETH derivative they were exposed to. This approach mitigated derivative-specific tail risks while preserving flexibility in overall strategy management.

Participants could structure their hedge based on their broader portfolio objectives. Using ETH as collateral allowed them to hedge derivative-specific risks while maintaining exposure to ETH price movements. Alternatively, using a stablecoin as collateral provided protection against both ETH directional exposure and derivative-specific tail risks.

Case Study: Hedging USDe Exposure

In 2024, a common strategy involved holding USDe, Ethena's stablecoin, to accumulate points that would eventually convert into tokens, generating additional returns. Similar to ETH LRTs, USDe lacked derivative markets for shorting due to its theoretical parity with 1 USD. This absence of derivatives made hedging tail risks more challenging.

Participants could mitigate USDe-specific risks by borrowing USDe against USDC on a money market, preferably one utilizing an exchange rate oracle.

This hedging strategy applies to any asset where participants face overexposure within a broader portfolio. As discussed in the diversification section, even with multiple strategies in place, concentration risk could arise if all collateral was tied to a single stablecoin. Hedging such assets through money markets provides a way to manage exposure effectively, even in the absence of perpetual contracts or other derivatives.

Case Study: Using USDe as Collateral to Hedge

For participants holding USDe, money markets provide a way to hedge exposure to unrelated assets, such as ETH, using USDe as collateral. This is particularly useful because most perpetual platforms do not accept USDe as margin for shorting other assets. By leveraging money markets, participants can manage risk effectively while maintaining the benefits of their USDe position.

USDe has recently experienced rapid adoption, expanding its partnerships and integrations. It is now accepted as collateral on derivative platforms like ByBit, though this strategy remains applicable to any emerging asset with similar characteristics.

Note that market efficiency typically aligns the borrowing rate of an asset with its expected return. As a result, hedging an asset by borrowing it often comes at a cost that offsets most or all of the asset's yield—unless the market is mispriced. If the yield is underestimated, a participant can secure a profitable hedge. Conversely, an overestimated yield may lead to a net loss despite the hedge.

2.3) Intrinsic Lending Yields

On-chain money markets present numerous opportunities for asymmetric yield when used effectively. While lending rates generally follow market-wide demand for leverage, individual markets operate under unique conditions, leading to inefficiencies that can be exploited.

This section explores how participants can optimize lending yields through blue-chip platforms like Aave and Compound, isolated markets such as Morpho and Euler, and vault products designed to automate yield maximization.

What Determines Rates?

At its core, interest rates for lending in DeFi are shaped by the demand for leverage. Typically, lending rates rise during bullish market conditions, where demand for leverage peaks, and fall during bearish periods, when leverage demand wanes.

While broad market demand determines the base lending rates that markets tend to stabilize around, individual market rates are directly influenced by their utilization rates and the IRMs they employ.

Markets are not always efficient in aligning these rates with broader averages, often deviating due to specific dynamics. For instance, constraints, like capped TVL, can limit lend-side liquidity and disrupt equilibrium, leading to specific markets displaying higher-than-average interest rates.

Blue-Chip Lending: Compound and Aave

Compound and Aave are foundational protocols in DeFi, recognized for their risk-averse and battle-tested design, offering stable and reliable lending yields. Although these platforms represent the lowest-risk money markets in DeFi, zero-risk is unattainable. There is always an inherent risk of protocol exploits, despite no such incidents occurring during their operational history.

Major stablecoin lending yields on these platforms typically represent the current risk-free rate of DeFi. The risk-free rate is the baseline interest rate, which more exotic protocols and collateral are benchmarked against, to determine a premium depending on relative perceived risk. Historically, these rates range from 1 to 15%+ APY, depending on market conditions.

Blue-chip lending is the favored venue to align leading and lagging rates in DeFi through rate arbitrage, as participants want minimal platform risk and maximum liquidity. As seen previously, if stablecoin A offers a higher lending yield than the borrow rate of stablecoin B, while it is not perceived as more risky, participants will borrow stablecoin B and sell it for stablecoin A, which they will lend.

Isolated Markets: Morpho and Euler

Isolated markets such as Morpho and Euler provide lending opportunities for assets that are not yet available on platforms like Aave or Compound. These markets tend to be the ones generating outlier returns due to unique demand dynamics for newer assets that may be running a points campaign or other forms of incentives.

For example, the Resolv market on Euler offered 20–30% APY for lending USDC over an extended period. This high yield resulted from a significant demand for leverage on Resolv assets, where participants borrowed and sold USDC into Resolv assets to farm points, and a TVL cap.

The TVL cap restricted the ability of the market to lower the utilization rate—and consequently the lending rate—by increasing lend-side liquidity. Another way to reduce the utilization rate would have been decreasing the amount borrowed, but borrowers were largely insensitive to rising borrowing rates, confident that the rewards from farming Resolv points would far exceed the borrowing costs.

As a result, the lending rates did not normalize and remained above market averages until the TVL cap was raised/removed.

Vault Products

Achieving optimal lending yields involves outperforming the market rate by rebalancing between protocols to capitalize on inefficiencies in liquidity distribution across DeFi platforms. This process requires market knowledge, constant monitoring, and awareness of several data points for market health. Vault products emerged to automate this effort, offering users a simplified way to maximize returns across multiple protocols.

SuperUSDC is an example of a vault specifically designed to optimize lending rates by aggregating yield opportunities across major money markets. It strategically allocates funds into markets experiencing utilization spikes; for example, if a specific market offers 25% lending rates for USDC (e.g., Euler Resolv market), the vault directs deposits there until the rates normalize.

Vaults are not only highly beneficial for their users but also for the entire DeFi ecosystem. Increased adoption of these products could have significant second-order effects, such as normalizing borrow rates across the lending ecosystem, enhancing liquidity available for leveraging exotic collateral, reducing the frequency of interest rate spikes, and improving overall accessibility to leverage. These impacts would contribute to a more efficient and stable DeFi landscape.

3. <u>Liquidity Provision Strategies</u>

Liquidity provision is often presented as a passive income strategy, but in reality, it is one of the most nuanced, unintuitive, and poorly understood activities in DeFi. It is more akin to actively managing a trading position than holding a fixed-income instrument or interest-bearing asset.

LP performance depends on three factors (in addition to underlying asset performance, if not hedged):

    i. **Impermanent Loss (IL):** The value leak of consistently trading at bad prices.

    ii. **Fee Revenue:** The compensation LPs receive from trading activity, which varies based on exchange growth and user activity.

    iii. **Rewards:** Additional incentives provided by protocols, often structured through liquidity mining or points-based campaigns.

These factors are volatile, complex, and often misleadingly advertised. Understanding them is critical for constructing an efficient liquidity provision strategy, especially within delta-neutral frameworks.

3.1) Impermanent Loss: A Structural Issue

IL is one of the most misunderstood risks in liquidity provision. It is often presented as a temporary and manageable downside to AMM participation, but in reality, it is a fundamental structural flaw that makes AMMs inherently less efficient than traditional order books.

Unlike standard trading risks, where losses occur due to poor market timing or directional miscalculations, IL is systematically extracted from LPs over time. This occurs because AMMs operate with rigid pricing structures that allow arbitrageurs to exploit LPs' positions, consistently leading to negative-EV trades.

What Is Impermanent Loss?

IL occurs when the price of assets in an AMM pool moves away from their original ratio at the time of deposit. Because AMMs automatically rebalance pools through their pricing curves, LPs end up holding a larger proportion of the underperforming asset while traders extract profits from price disparities. The term "impermanent" suggests that these losses are reversible if asset prices return to their initial state.

Consider an LP who provides equal-value liquidity in ETH and USDC at a $2,000 ETH price. If ETH rises to $3,000, arbitrage traders buy ETH from the pool at a discount until the ratio reflects the new market price. By the time the LP withdraws, they hold fewer ETH and more USDC than they initially deposited, leading to a lower final portfolio value compared with simply holding the assets outside the pool.

The Structural Issue of Impermanent Loss

IL can be seen as the systematic execution of bad trades by LPs. Unlike market makers in traditional order books who adjust bid-ask spreads dynamically, LPs in AMMs are forced to offer liquidity at predefined ratios, unable to react to price changes in real time. This creates an asymmetric risk-reward structure:

- **Passive, Non-Adjustable Quotes:** In an order book, a market maker places bids and asks based on real-time data and can adjust spreads to reduce losses. In an AMM, LPs are bound to the algorithm's curve.

- **Arbitrage Exploitation:** As soon as market prices deviate, arbitrageurs extract value by trading against outdated pool prices, locking in risk-free gains at the LPs' expense.

- **High Fees as Compensation:** To offset IL, AMMs impose higher transaction fees than order book-based exchanges. However, this increases friction for traders and reduces competitive efficiency.

Understanding the Impermanent Loss Curve

IL scales non-linearly with price movements. Small fluctuations result in minor losses, but as price divergence increases, IL grows exponentially. For example:

- A 2x price increase in one asset leads to 5.7% IL.

- A 10x price increase in one asset leads to 45% IL.

Some market conditions worsen IL and reduce LP profitability. LPs must recognize these factors to mitigate their risks effectively.

- **Uncorrelated Asset Pairs:** Greater divergence in asset prices leads to higher IL.

- **Low Volume and Low Fee Tiers:** Without sufficient trading volume or higher fees, LPs may struggle to offset IL losses.

Takeaways

IL is not a temporary inconvenience—it is a fundamental risk of AMMs that stems from their structural inefficiencies. LPs are systematically disadvantaged compared to arbitrageurs, and while some mechanisms can reduce IL, they cannot eliminate it. The only way to achieve sustainable profitability as an LP is by ensuring that fee revenue and rewards consistently exceed IL losses. Otherwise, liquidity provision becomes a long-term losing game, with LPs unknowingly subsidizing traders who take advantage of predictable price inefficiencies.

3.2) Fees and Rewards: The Liquidity Provider's Compensation

LPs in AMMs earn fees and incentives, but the profitability of these mechanisms is often overstated. Fees are designed to compensate LPs for providing liquidity and absorbing risks, such as IL. The sustainability of these earnings is highly dependent on trading volume and market conditions. Additional incentives, such as liquidity mining rewards and points-based incentive programs, can enhance returns temporarily but introduce new risks, including market distortions and liquidity migration when incentives disappear. In the face of reduced fees and incentives, LPs face not only reduced profitability, but also potential losses.

Liquidity Provider Role in Automated Market Makers

When LPs contribute to AMM pools, they take on a role similar to traditional market makers, but with critical disadvantages. Unlike market makers in CEXs, who can actively adjust their bid-ask spreads, LPs in AMMs provide liquidity passively across a price curve. This lack of flexibility forces LPs into a suboptimal position where they are constantly arbitraged against by traders as price evolves. Fees and incentives are designed to offset these risks.

Fee Calculation and Revenue Potential

The effectiveness of fee revenue depends on two major factors:

i. **Trading Volume vs. Total Value Locked (TVL):** A high volume-to-TVL ratio is necessary for LPs to earn meaningful fee income. If a pool has a large amount of capital but low trading activity, LPs will generate little revenue while still being exposed to IL.

ii. **Fee Structure:** The revenue generated is a product of the fee tier of the pool. Pools incurring higher risk (e.g., more volatile and less correlated assets) will have higher fee tiers to offset the downside.

The standard AMM fee structure varies by protocol:

- **Uniswap v2:** 0.3% per trade, distributed to LPs.

- **Uniswap v3:** Variable fee tiers (0.05%, 0.30%, 1%), allowing LPs to customize their exposure.

- **Curve Finance:** Optimized for stablecoin pairs with lower fees (~0.04%) but higher volume.

The Role of Incentives

Because LPs cannot dynamically adjust their quotes like traditional market makers, they are bleeding value to arbitrageurs. To make up for this, they have to charge substantial fees compared to an order book model, which even uninformed retail traders will have to pay. The only way to counteract this is to have an external source of payment for LPs that helps compensate IL without charging unreasonable fees. That is the role of incentives. Historically, incentives have taken two forms:

- **Liquidity Mining:** Protocols distribute native tokens to LPs as an incentive to deposit liquidity. While this boosts short-term APYs, it can create unsustainable yield cycles where TVL drops sharply once rewards decline.

- **Points-Based Incentives:** Some protocols offer points instead of tokens, delaying emissions while still incentivizing liquidity. This strategy allows projects to retain control over future tokenomics but adds uncertainty for LPs who cannot directly value their rewards.

Takeaways

Being a liquidity provider is essentially a bet that fees and incentives will outpace IL. It's a guess as to what the volume-TVL ratio of an exchange will be going forward. You're not only making a bet on the two asset prices, but also on the relative price of the assets and the health/growth of the liquidity pool itself.

3.3) Liquidity Provision Within Delta-Neutral Strategies

Liquidity provision can serve as a way to generate yield on spot assets that are part of a broader delta-neutral strategy. Unlike lending strategies, for example, LP positions require continuous risk assessment due to IL and fluctuating fee revenue. While delta-neutral traders seek to hedge directional exposure, LP strategies introduce complexities that prevent perfect hedging. The constant rebalancing of an AMM pool results in ongoing asset adjustments, making it hard/expensive to perfectly neutralize the delta.

Historical Fee Trends

Many platforms display fee APRs based on the last twenty-four hours, projected over a year, which can be misleading. A more accurate approach is to analyze weekly or monthly historical fee trends, which provide a clearer picture of long-term profitability.

Total Value Locked Growth Impact

The TVL in a pool determines how LP rewards are distributed. When TVL increases, more liquidity enters the pool, which leads to a dilution of yield, since trading fees must be distributed among a larger group of LPs. If TVL rises without a corresponding increase in trading volume, it leads to declining profitability, as each LP receives a smaller share of the fees.

Volume Growth and Trading Activity

Higher trading volume generates more fees, leading to improved LP returns. The volume-to-TVL ratio is a crucial metric for determining LP profitability. A higher ratio indicates more active trading and a greater accumulation of fees relative to the liquidity supplied.

Price Volatility Considerations

- Short-term volatility is beneficial—frequent price fluctuations increase trading activity, leading to more fees.

- Long-term divergence is harmful—when paired assets in a pool diverge significantly in price, IL risk increases.

Managing Liquidity Provision in a Delta-Neutral Portfolio

- LP positions should be used in combination with hedging instruments, such as perpetual futures or options, to offset some of the directional exposure.

- The sustainability of an LP strategy depends on balancing IL risk with sufficient fee revenue and incentives.

- Effective LP management requires constant monitoring of pool-specific factors, including protocol incentives, market depth, and trading activity.

Takeaways

Liquidity provision can be a useful yield-generation tool within delta-neutral strategies, but it is far from passive income. The constant rebalancing in AMMs makes perfect hedging impossible, so LPs must ensure that fee revenues and incentives compensate for IL. High trading volume and short-term volatility can improve returns, while growing TVL without proportional trading activity dilutes yield. Successful LP strategies require ongoing monitoring, careful asset selection, and a clear understanding of the exchange dynamics that drive profitability.

4. Staking

Staking is a fundamental mechanism in PoS blockchains for validating transactions; this is blockchain-level staking. Staking can also refer to protocol-level (or application-level) staking.

Protocol-level staking refers to locking tokens within a protocol to gain various benefits, such as yield, governance rights, or enhanced utility. Unlike blockchain-level staking, this does not contribute to network security; it is simply a financial commitment to access benefits.

Both forms of staking play a crucial role in aligning incentives and generating utility for token holders, with distinct mechanisms and purposes driving their adoption.

4.1) Protocol Staking Rewards

Protocols in DeFi offer various staking reward mechanisms to incentivize token holders to lock their tokens. Often, these rewards include multipliers for selecting longer lock-up periods, increasing returns based on commitment duration. While these rewards vary widely in structure and sustainability, they all aim to align incentives and provide value to token holders.

Emissions-Based Rewards

Some protocols reward stakers through token emissions, distributing additional tokens derived from inflation. For example, SushiSwap's xSushi mechanism rewards stakers with a share of Sushi emissions. While this approach can attract participants in the short term, it is often unsustainable, as it relies heavily on continued token issuance, which can dilute value over time.

Revenue-Based Rewards

Revenue-based rewards provide a more sustainable model by distributing a portion of the protocol's revenue to stakers. Ethena, for instance, redistributes the revenue generated to staked tokens (sUSDe). This approach aligns rewards with the protocol's performance, offering a more stable and sustainable return to participants.

Voting Rights

Staking can grant participants voting rights, empowering them to influence key protocol decisions. For example, Curve's veCRV system allows stakers to direct CRV emissions to specific liquidity pools, making governance a valuable tool. The challenge for protocols is ensuring that these voting rights are valuable.

Functional Benefits

Some protocols offer practical advantages to stakers, such as reduced fees, allocation opportunities, or improved APY on specific pools. However, a potential downside of such an approach is that these benefits are only valuable to users who actively engage with the protocol, limiting the broader appeal of the token.

Mixed Reward Structures

Many protocols combine multiple reward types to create more complex and innovative incentive systems. Pendle, for instance, rewards stakers with both voting rights and APY boosts on select positions. This hybrid approach allows protocols to attain a more versatile compromise between the pros and cons of each option.

4.2) Evaluating Protocol Staking Yield

Evaluating the yield from protocol staking requires a comprehensive understanding of both direct and indirect returns, as well as the market dynamics that influence these rewards. By carefully assessing the components of staking yields, participants can determine the potential profitability and risks associated with staking opportunities.

Estimating Real Returns

Staking yields can be broken down into direct and indirect returns. Direct returns include token emissions or revenue distributions offered by the protocol. Indirect returns stem from benefits such as monetizable voting rights or advantages when using the protocol, such as fee reductions or allocation boosts. By combining these factors, participants can estimate the potential APR of staking. Unlike blockchain staking rewards, protocol-based rewards tend to be less stable, but this inherent instability is what creates opportunities for participants to capitalize on.

Market Efficiency

Market efficiency plays a significant role in determining the real return of staking opportunities. High staking yields typically attract more participants, leading to a dilution of returns through an increase in the staking rate and the token's price.

Despite this, opportunities can arise when the current or future returns are underestimated by the market, creating undervalued staking opportunities. This most often happens when returns are indirect or harder to quantify in real time, making the market less efficient in normalizing these returns.

Liquidity and Capital Efficiency

Evaluating the liquidity and capital efficiency of the staking position is critical before entering the position.

i. Determine whether the locked position has tradable receipt tokens associated with it, enabling an early exit before the term ends by selling it on the secondary market.

ii. Assess the liquidity, market depth, and illiquidity discount (price compared to the unstaked version of the token).

iii. Evaluate the composability of the token; for example, tokens with active lending markets enable leverage, enhancing capital efficiency and creating opportunities for higher returns or complementary strategies.

A well-structured staking position emphasizes liquidity and capital efficiency, minimizing the risk of being locked into an illiquid asset while maximizing potential returns. Highly liquid receipt tokens allow for greater flexibility, while composability enhances the utility of staked assets by enabling leverage and integration into broader DeFi strategies.

4.3) Staking Within Delta-Neutral Strategies

Delta-neutral staking combines the benefits of staking with the risk management principles of delta-neutral strategies, allowing participants to isolate the staking yield from the staking asset. Achieving delta neutrality while staking requires careful consideration of hedging instruments, liquidity, and the volatility of the underlying asset.

Managing Volatility

Liquidity and volatility of the staking asset are major risk factors in delta-neutral strategies. Locked positions with no secondary market liquidity pose significant risks if the asset's price rises dramatically. Without the ability to sell or adjust positions, participants may face challenges in maintaining their hedges.

For example, consider this situation where the hedge fails due to volatility:

i. **Context:** The participant locks the asset for one year to earn staking rewards and opens a short of equal size on perpetual futures to remain delta-neutral. Funding rates are currently positive, meaning that long positions pay short positions in the perpetual market for this asset.

ii. **Price Doubles:** The price of the asset doubles, requiring the participant to add margin to keep the hedge open.

iii. **Further Doubles Again:** The price of the asset doubles again (now 4x from the starting price), and the participant cannot provide additional margin to maintain the hedge. The short position must be closed to avoid liquidation, leaving the participant exposed to price fluctuations for the remainder of the lock-up period.

iv. **Lock-Up Completion:** By the end of the lock-up period, the price of the asset has returned to its starting level (e.g., $1 to $4 to $1). The participant has lost 75% of their capital due to interim price movements and the failed hedge.

This example highlights the risks of illiquid locked positions and the importance of having sufficient liquidity for additional margin in such cases, especially during volatile market conditions.

Composability and Capital Efficiency

The ability to integrate staked assets into various protocols unlocks yield opportunities far beyond the staking rewards themselves. Liquid staked assets can be leveraged, used as collateral, or deployed in liquidity provision; it becomes an active component of a broader strategy rather than a passive position. Participants can borrow against it to hedge risk, amplify returns through leverage, or provide liquidity to earn additional fees. These interconnected strategies allow capital to work continuously, optimizing efficiency across multiple DeFi markets.

5. __Counterparty Vaults__

CPVs blend liquidity provision and staking, allowing users to deposit assets on a platform, akin to staking, while those assets are used for market-making, akin to liquidity provision. CPVs pool capital to provide liquidity for decentralized perpetual markets, acting as the counterparty to traders.

These vaults generate revenue from trading fees and trader losses, capitalizing on the historical tendency of traders to underperform as a group due to fees, funding costs, and poor strategy. Unlike traditional market-making, CPVs offer a passive, accessible way for users to participate in liquidity provision without requiring advanced trading expertise.

CPVs operate through different mechanisms, such as proprietary market-making algorithms (e.g., Hyperliquid's HLP). As DeFi evolves and DEXs are gaining market share, CPVs are becoming a cornerstone for users seeking diversified, passive yield opportunities while enabling deeper liquidity in decentralized markets.

5.1) Key Features and Benefits

CPVs offer a range of unique features and benefits, making them an attractive option for participants in the DeFi ecosystem. By democratizing the market-making, liquidation processes and enhancing the stability of trading platforms, CPVs have introduced opportunities for LPs, platforms, and traders:

- **Transparency:** Decentralized platforms offering CPVs often provide detailed information on vault composition, fee structures, and performance metrics. This transparency allows participants to make informed decisions, reducing information asymmetry and building trust in the system. Additionally, many CPVs operate on open-source protocols, enabling users to audit the code and verify its integrity.

- **Capital Efficiency:** Through composability, CPVs enable efficient capital allocation by pooling resources and deploying them across a wide range of trading activities while providing receipt tokens that can allow the depositor to remain in control of their liquid funds while they are being used for the CPV strategy. CPV tokens representing ownership stakes can be used as collateral in lending protocols or as components in yield optimization strategies.

- **Negative Beta Characteristics:** CPVs tend to exhibit negative beta, meaning their performance is inversely correlated with broader market trends. This characteristic arises because CPVs profit from trader losses, which often increase during periods of heightened market volatility, especially to the downside. As a result, CPVs can serve as a valuable diversification tool in a portfolio, reducing overall risk and enhancing stability.

5.2) Mechanics and Operation

CPVs function as the backbone of trading platforms, facilitating market efficiency while providing opportunities for LPs to earn yield. Their operation is driven by several interconnected components and mechanisms that ensure the smooth execution of trades and the accrual of profits. Below, we break down the core aspects of CPV mechanics and operations:

- **Asset Composition:** CPVs can be designed to accept single-asset deposits or multi-asset deposits. Single-asset vaults (such as Hyperliquid's HLP) simplify management but may introduce higher concentration exposure to the token, which is often mitigated by using stablecoins such as USDC as the primary asset. On the other hand, multi-asset vaults (such as Jupiter's JLP) diversify exposure and provide greater liquidity for a broader range of trading pairs. They typically contain about 50% in volatile assets and 50% in various stablecoins.

- **Oracle Integration:** Price data is critical for the operation of the platform that supports CPVs. Oracles serve as the source of truth for asset prices and, consequently, funding rates, ensuring trades are executed at fair market values. For instance, Jupiter perpetuals rely on oracle prices to determine asset prices, while Hyperliquid perpetuals use them to calculate funding payments, which serve as a mechanism to keep prices in line with fair market values. Reliable oracle integration is essential to prevent manipulation and ensure accurate pricing.

- **Liquidation Execution:** CPVs are often responsible for executing liquidations when traders' collateral falls below maintenance margin requirements. By performing liquidations efficiently, CPVs help maintain platform solvency while earning additional revenue from liquidation fees. Once again, an activity that is traditionally not accessible to all market participants.

- **Fee Accrual:** CPVs capture a significant portion of the fees generated by the platform. These fees typically include trading fees and liquidation fees. Over time, the fee accrual serves as a steady income stream for CPV participants.

- **Trader PNL Accrual:** Since CPVs act as the counterparty to all trades on the platform, they capture profits from traders' net losses. This structural advantage arises from the statistical tendency of traders, as a group, to underperform due to factors like poor strategy, high leverage, and market inefficiencies.

- **Strategy Variations:** CPVs employ different strategies depending on the platform. Some vaults operate transparently, simply taking the opposite side of trades, while others may employ more complex market-making strategies, such as hedging exposure to reduce directional risk or enhancing returns by reinvesting idle collateral.

5.3) How to Incorporate Counterparty Vaults into a Set of Delta-Neutral Strategies

CPVs have become an essential component of delta-neutral strategies in DeFi. By providing stable yield and acting as a counterbalance to market volatility, CPVs enable portfolio managers to enhance returns while minimizing risk. This section explores how CPVs integrate into delta-neutral portfolios and the advantages they bring.

Role of Counterparty Vaults in Delta-Neutral Strategies

CPVs can serve as a stable yield source, generating consistent returns through trading fees, liquidation fees, and traders' aggregate losses. This reliability makes them a cornerstone for delta-neutral portfolios, which prioritize minimizing directional exposure while seeking stable profits. Additionally, the returns generated by CPVs often exhibit negative beta characteristics, meaning they can offset potential losses from other strategies during periods of market stress or heightened volatility.

By incorporating CPVs, participants can reduce exposure to market fluctuations without relying solely on traditional hedging techniques.

This creates a more resilient portfolio structure capable of weathering diverse market conditions.

Successful integration of CPVs into delta-neutral portfolios requires careful allocation and balance with other strategies, such as arbitrage and hedging. For example, while CPVs offer stable yields, they may not provide the rapid capital turnover associated with some arbitrage strategies. Combining CPVs with arbitrage opportunities allows portfolios to benefit from both long-term stability and short-term gains.

Hedging Multi-Asset Counterparty Vaults

Multi-asset CPVs present a unique challenge for fully delta-neutral strategies due to their evolving exposure to volatile assets. For instance, CPVs like Jupiter's JLP, which targets a composition of 44% SOL, 10% ETH, 11% WBTC, 26% USDC, and 9% USDT, inherently carry positive delta due to the volatile components. To neutralize this exposure, portfolio managers can dynamically hedge these assets, leveraging volatility models to guide rebalancing decisions.

A practical example involves using platforms like Drift to hedge the volatile assets held by JLP. By depositing JLP into Drift, managers can hedge exposure to SOL, ETH, and BTC efficiently while utilizing the same platform for collateral management.

While this approach ensures that the portfolio remains delta-neutral despite the underlying volatility of the CPV, it also introduces new counterparty risk. Instead of being exposed to JLP's delta, the strategy is now exposed to Drift counterparty risk, which is necessary to create the hedge.

Risk Management in Portfolio Integration

Integrating CPVs into delta-neutral portfolios involves managing inherent risks effectively. Diversification across multiple CPVs—each with unique asset compositions, strategies, and risk profiles—helps mitigate idiosyncratic risks associated with individual platforms. For instance, combining CPVs like Hyperliquid's HLP, GMX's GLP, and Jupiter's JLP provides exposure to diverse mechanisms, blockchains, and strategies, reducing reliance on any single system.

Additionally, participants must evaluate trade-offs between returns and risks. Generally, more reliable CPVs will have higher TVL, which will lower the yield. Higher-yield CPVs might carry elevated risks, such as oracle dependency, counterparty exposure, or strategy risk. Allocating smaller portions of the portfolio to higher-risk CPVs can enhance returns while maintaining a strong risk profile.

Takeaways

CPVs have become a cornerstone of delta-neutral strategies, contributing stable returns and diversifying risk. Their composability within DeFi protocols allows for seamless integration into broader portfolio strategies. When combined with tools like arbitrage and hedging, CPVs enhance resilience and facilitate sophisticated risk-managed constructions.

By effectively integrating CPVs, participants can capitalize on their unique characteristics while maintaining a disciplined approach to risk management. This ensures that CPVs remain a reliable and strategic component of DeFi portfolios.

6. <u>Incentives</u>

Crypto projects are in a constant battle for adoption. Whether they are blockchains or protocols, the goal is always to drive growth and engagement. To achieve this, they leverage their tokens to incentivize user participation and activity.

The landscape of incentives has evolved dramatically since DeFi Summer in 2020, when liquidity mining—using token distributions to reward participation—was the primary method of attracting users. By late 2023, points-based campaigns emerged as the dominant strategy.

For users, these evolving mechanisms open the door to numerous opportunities for enhanced returns. By understanding and leveraging these strategies, participants can achieve substantial outperformance.

6.1) Token Incentives — Liquidity Mining

Liquidity mining has been a cornerstone of DeFi since its inception, providing a straightforward mechanism for protocols to attract users by distributing tokens as rewards. Although its prominence has diminished with the rise of points-based incentives, liquidity mining remains a powerful tool for blockchains and protocols with existing tokens to boost adoption and engagement.

Current State of Liquidity Mining

Today, liquidity mining is primarily used by projects that allocate tokens from their treasury or community pool to incentivize participation. For example, Mantle (a blockchain) is distributing 1M MNT (~$1.1M) over two months to users of Merchant Moe, its native DEX. These rewards aim to increase activity on the platform and deepen liquidity in trading pairs.

Unique Opportunities

In some cases, liquidity mining creates scenarios where dynamics are heavily altered, such as users effectively being paid to borrow. This can occur when the incentives provided for borrowing exceed the interest rates charged. For instance, on Compound's Mantle deployment, the net borrow interest rate is currently negative: the borrow cost is 2.57%, while Compound incentives amount to 3.95%; the user is therefore paid 1.38% APR to borrow assets. Such opportunities allow participants to execute strategies such as looping while earning a profit on borrowed assets.

Analysis

One of the key advantages of liquidity mining is its transparency. Participants can clearly see the APR offered by the incentives and calculate their expected returns with precision. This simplicity makes it easier for users to evaluate opportunities and integrate them into their strategies.

However, this is a double-edged sword. Market efficiency has improved significantly since the early days of DeFi, meaning that attractive APRs are quickly diluted as more participants enter the market. High-return opportunities tend to be short-lived as the influx of liquidity normalizes returns relative to the risks involved.

Liquidity mining continues to offer valuable opportunities for participants and remains an important part of DeFi's incentive structure. While its scope has narrowed, its straightforward nature and potential for unique scenarios ensure its relevance in the evolving DeFi ecosystem.

6.2) Points-Based Incentives — Hidden Liquidity Mining

Points-based incentives have become a leading strategy for attracting users to DeFi. These campaigns enable projects to incentivize participation while deferring token emissions, offering greater flexibility and control over reward structures. By maintaining control over tokenomics and promising future rewards, points-based incentives have reshaped how projects engage with their users.

Power Skew Toward Projects

Points-based incentives differ significantly from token-based rewards in their structure and implications:

- **Lack of Transparency:** Projects typically do not disclose critical details, such as the duration of points-based campaigns, the conversion rate of points to tokens, or even tokenomics. This opacity allows projects to adapt these parameters far longer than previously.

- **Uncertain Returns:** Users who invest time and resources to earn points face significant challenges in estimating their returns, which are not only uncertain but also delayed. For instance, revisiting the negative net interest rates for borrowing on money markets discussed earlier, while token incentives might exceed the borrow interest rate, participants cannot be certain of this in advance and must cover the associated fees upfront.

Analysis

While points-based incentives heavily favor projects, they also create unique opportunities for users. The lack of transparency and uncertainty surrounding these campaigns reduces market efficiency, leaving high-return opportunities available for longer periods. For sophisticated participants, this opacity presents an edge, enabling them to identify and exploit undervalued opportunities.

A notable example is Ethena's Shard season one. When Ethena publicly launched, it incentivized users to participate with Ethena Shards (essentially points) to ensure explosive growth and adoption. Because the yield was not clearly expressed, the market was inefficient and did not normalize the rate of return, and when season one ended, early participants walked out with an ROI of ~150% in ~45 days, which represents a mind-blowing ~1,300% internal rate of return (IRR) over this period.

6.3) Taking Advantage of Points-Based Incentives

Points-based incentives offer substantial opportunities for participants who can accurately estimate and capitalize on their hidden participation APR. By analyzing key factors and executing effectively, users can optimize their returns in these opaque reward systems.

The primary goal when analyzing points-based campaigns is to estimate the hidden participation APR, which reflects the profitability of participating in a campaign. Three main factors influence the potential APR:

- **Participation Levels:** The number of users participating directly impacts the dilution of rewards.

- **Fully Diluted Valuation (FDV) at Launch:** The project's launch FDV is crucial to determine the value of the distributed tokens.

- **Supply Allocation to Airdrop:** Understanding how much of the total supply may be allocated to the incentive campaign allows for a more accurate calculation.

Estimating Hidden APR

The hidden APR refers to the real return rate of participating in the protocol, which will only be measurable after the fact, when all rewards have been distributed. To estimate the hidden APR, participants should follow these steps:

i. **Estimate Launch FDV:** Analyze market conditions and comparable projects to predict the likely FDV of the project at launch.

ii. **Estimate Supply Allocated to Airdrop:** Review publicly available information or infer from similar campaigns to gauge the proportion of total supply set aside for points distribution.

iii. **Estimate Total Points Distributed:** Calculate or approximate the total number of points likely to be distributed during the campaign based on current participation and rate of increase.

iv. **Estimate the Value of One Point:** Divide the estimated airdrop supply value by the total points to derive the approximate value of each point.

v. **Convert Points Return to USD Return and APR:** Translate the estimated points earned into USD value, then calculate the corresponding APR based on the time and capital involved.

Execution

Effectively executing a points-based incentive strategy requires managing uncertainties and adapting to varying levels of campaign clarity:

- **Opaque Points Distribution:** When distribution details are unclear, focus on behaviors that benefit the project or are challenging to fake/duplicate.

- **Opaque Timeline:** Prepare for indefinite timelines by balancing participation across multiple campaigns to mitigate opportunity costs.

- **Sybils Often Win:** A Sybil strategy involves splitting a large account into many smaller ones to trick the project into distributing rewards as if they were going to multiple unique users. Due to the nature of distribution curves and the necessity for projects to incorporate some sort of minimum allocation for small users (the goal of an airdrop remains user acquisition and marketing), Sybil strategies often receive more rewards and are rarely punished if done properly.

With consistent and effective analysis, participants can uncover and capitalize on lucrative opportunities within points incentive campaigns. Understanding the interplay between opacity and market inefficiency is key to achieving outsized returns in these scenarios.

7. <u>Yield Trading Applied</u>

On-chain yield trading provides a powerful tool for enhancing delta-neutral strategies by stabilizing cash flows and managing risks associated with variable yields. By tokenizing future interest rates, traders can separate principal and yield exposure, allowing for more precise risk control and optimized returns.

This section explores how yield-trading components, such as PTs and YTs, can be used to secure fixed income, express views on future yields, and structure advanced strategies. This section will cover methods for utilizing PTs and YTs, leveraging tokenized yields in delta-neutral portfolios, and managing the associated risks effectively.

7.1) Expressing Directional Bias on Yields

By utilizing PTs, YTs, or providing liquidity for both, users can align their strategies with anticipated yield movements and other portfolio exposure. These positions provide flexibility to hedge, speculate, or optimize returns based on the market environment.

Foundational Scenarios

If yields are expected to decrease, participants should buy PTs to secure the current implied yield.

- This is equivalent to swapping floating rates for a fixed rate. By purchasing PTs, the holder secures a predetermined return that remains stable regardless of future market fluctuations. It is important to understand that the yield is fixed and guaranteed if the PT is held to maturity, but its value does not necessarily increase in a linear fashion.

If yields are expected to increase, participants should buy YTs to gain leveraged exposure to rising yields.

- YTs provide leverage-like exposure to yield movements, amplifying gains when yields rise. This makes them an attractive option for participants expecting an increase in yield rates and looking to maximize potential returns. However, unlike PTs, which can only forgo gains but never incur losses, holding YTs (even to maturity) carries the risk of negative returns if yields fall short of expectations.

If yields are expected to remain stable: Participants should provide liquidity for the asset's PT/YT pool to earn additional yield through trading fees and market activity.

- Providing liquidity for both PTs and YTs replicates exposure to the full underlying asset without directional yield bias. Additionally, it enables participants to earn trading fees by facilitating transactions for other yield speculators. This type of liquidity pool is protected from significant IL thanks to optimized AMMs, making it a stable option for yield-neutral strategies.

Takeaways

Whether locking in fixed yields with PTs, leveraging YTs for amplified exposure, or utilizing LP strategies for additional returns, tokenized yield trading offers diverse opportunities to optimize performance. These approaches create a structured foundation for more advanced strategies, allowing participants to fine-tune their exposure to varying market conditions.

7.2) Advanced Principal Token Utilization

PTs provide a powerful tool for market participants to take the opposite side of an overconfident market or to secure future cash flows. They offer a low-risk way to generate predictable returns (especially when no leverage is involved), making them attractive to risk-averse investors and structured strategies. By strategically selecting entry points and leveraging inefficiencies in market sentiment, PT holders can lock in attractive fixed yields while avoiding exposure to fluctuating interest rates.

Being the Counterparty to an Overconfident Market

Markets often misprice implied yields, particularly when speculative participants inflate demand for certain assets. Points farming campaigns, for instance, can lead to situations where users aggressively buy yield-generating assets, artificially increasing their yield expectations.

For example, if market sentiment drives PT discounts to imply a yield far above reasonable expectations (e.g., USD0++ rewards farming pushing implied yields to 50%+ APY), this presents an opportunity. A participant can purchase PTs at these discounted prices, locking in a fixed return while speculative traders take on the risk.

If the speculative activity subsides and yield expectations normalize, PT holders will have secured an attractive, stable rate with minimal downside. This strategy allows investors to capitalize on market inefficiencies and earn strong risk-adjusted returns without needing to speculate on future market conditions.

Securing Future Cash Flows for Stability

Fixed yields play a critical role in sophisticated strategies that require predictable returns. Many structured investment strategies require stabilized return volatility, aiming to respect certain metrics.

- PTs allow participants to lock in yield for a predetermined duration, providing clarity in expected returns.

- This is particularly useful for funds or strategies that need stable revenue generation and cannot afford full exposure to variable yield swings.

- For example, a strategy might require a fixed return component to offset unstable return exposure elsewhere in the portfolio.

By integrating PTs, investors can smooth out return fluctuations, enhancing capital efficiency and mitigating risk.

Timing Matters

While PTs offer predictable yields, the entry price at which they are acquired determines the final return. The implied yield of a PT is calculated based on the discount at which it trades relative to the underlying asset's value.

- Entering PT positions at favorable prices (e.g., during news events or after a surge in speculative demand) captures the highest implied yield, maximizing profitability without increasing risk exposure.

- Market participants who recognize catalysts that drive changes in perceived yield can strategically accumulate PTs to optimize their return profile.

For example, at the time of writing, Boyco's (an incentives market native to Berachain) imminent launch presents a unique arbitrage opportunity in the YT and PT markets. YTs are currently valued including the opportunity cost of holding them without earning points. However, once Berachain deposits go live and Boyco pre-deposit vaults start accumulating points, this discount should close, driving YT prices higher and PT prices lower, improving the implied yield.

With correct timing, sophisticated participants will be able to flip YTs into PTs after the launch and lock in profits now while securing favorable fixed rates later. That said, Boyco's launch timeline remains uncertain; it has been a moving target for a while. This uncertainty is precisely why the discount exists.

Takeaways

PTs offer a safe and effective way to secure fixed returns, particularly for those looking to stabilize cash flows or be the counterparty of market inefficiencies. By carefully considering entry prices and identifying mispricings driven by speculative behavior, participants can optimize their returns while minimizing risk. These strategies are foundational for more advanced interest rate plays in DeFi, allowing for structured, predictable income generation.

7.3) Advanced Yield Token Utilization

YTs are an exceptional liquidity management tool, providing a unique form of leverage for yield exposure. Unlike traditional leveraged strategies, YTs eliminate traditional risks such as liquidation risk and oracle dependency. Additionally, they help mitigate counterparty risk by reducing capital requirements, allowing for more balanced portfolio allocation and lower exposure concentration.

However, YTs are a double-edged sword. While they offer efficient yield leverage, they also introduce (yield) directional risk—if yield projections are incorrect, they can lead to significant capital losses. Understanding their mechanics and implications is crucial before incorporating them into a strategy.

Advantages of Yield Token Leveraged Exposure

- **No Borrow Costs:** Unlike traditional leveraged positions, YTs do not require borrowing funds, making them a more capital-efficient way to gain amplified yield exposure.

- **No Liquidation Risk:** Since YTs do not rely on collateralized borrowing, there is no risk of forced liquidation due to adverse price movements or lack of collateral management.

- **No Oracle Dependency:** Yield calculations are independent of external price feeds, eliminating exposure to oracle manipulation or inaccuracies.

Risks of Yield Token Leveraged Exposure

- **Directional Yield Bet:** YTs are inherently speculative—if yield expectations are incorrect, investors face significant capital losses.

- **Risk of Losses Exceeding Opportunity Cost:** Unlike borrowing-based leverage, which results in opportunity cost if yields underperform expectations, YTs can lead to actual losses.

Simplified Example

- A participant buys YTs at a 40% implied yield, meaning they expect the yield to exceed 40% for profitability.

- If the realized yield is only 20%, the participant does not earn or lose 20%—they lose half of their investment.

- Conversely, if the realized yield is 80%, the participant does not earn 40 or 80%—they double their investment.

Takeaways

YTs offer a powerful mechanism for liquidity management and yield optimization in DeFi. By leveraging their unique advantages, participants can gain amplified yield exposure while reducing capital concentration and counterparty risk. However, their directional nature means they must be used carefully, as incorrect yield projections can result in substantial losses. Proper risk assessment is essential when incorporating YTs into a broader yield strategy.

7.4) Looping Principal Tokens

PTs can be looped on certain money markets just like other assets, allowing participants to amplify exposure to fixed yields. However, unlike holding PTs to maturity for a guaranteed return, looping introduces variable costs that can impact profitability. Since borrowing rates fluctuate, looped PTs are not a true fixed-rate position, and their success depends on carefully managing cost dynamics.

Looped Principal Token Yield

Looping PTs follows a structured yield formula, identical to looping of other assets:

Position Yield = (Leverage × Collateral Yield) - ((Leverage - 1) × Borrow Cost)

The key distinction is that the collateral yield—determined by the PT's implied yield—is fixed. Profitability depends on the spread between the PT's implied yield and the prevailing borrow rate.

Risks of Looped Principal Tokens

While looping can amplify yield exposure, it also introduces risks that can erode profitability. If the borrow rate exceeds the PT's yield, the strategy becomes unprofitable and may need to be unwound prematurely to prevent continued losses.

Exiting the position early results in significant additional unwinding costs that can easily outweigh the generated returns:

- Swap fees when converting between assets to repay collateral.

- Looping protocol fees if applicable (e.g., Contango for flashloan looping).

- Potential slippage from selling PTs in illiquid markets.

- Potential losses from short-term PT price volatility at the time of sale (explained below).

Note that a 5x leveraged position, for example, magnifies costs significantly compared to base capital.

Losses from Short-Term Principal Token Price Volatility

Remember that PT yields are fixed only if held to maturity, but their market price fluctuates based on expectations. If an event occurs that leads the market to anticipate higher future yields than when the looped PT position was opened, the YT price will rise, causing the PT price to decline accordingly to reflect the newly agreed-upon implied yield.

As a result, exiting the position prematurely may mean selling PTs at a lower price than they were bought, realizing a loss.

Key Factors for Profitability

Effectively executing a PT looping strategy demands that participants master several key variables, including interest rate behavior and market liquidity. To navigate these complexities, they must consider:

- **Understanding the Interest Rate Model (IRM):** Predicting when and how borrow rates can change is essential to avoid unexpected cost increases.

- **Awareness of Deposit Caps:** If a deposit cap prevents borrow rates from rising, it can create asymmetric opportunities where yields remain favorable.

- **Oracle Risk Considerations:** Since looping introduces leverage, it also reintroduces traditional leverage risk. Therefore, it is crucial to verify which oracle (market rate vs.

exchange rate) is being used to avoid liquidations from mispriced assets.

- **Evaluating Returns and Costs:** Factoring in implied yield and maturity date compared to entry and exit fees of the position (e.g., swap fees and looping fees) is necessary to determine whether the expected yield outweighs incurred costs.

Takeaways

Looping PTs can be an effective yield optimization tool, but managing associated risks is essential to avoid eroding potential gains. A well-executed strategy requires forecasting interest rate movements, monitoring fees, and ensuring the cost-benefit ratio remains favorable. While PTs offer fixed yields, looping introduces variables that must be carefully navigated to maintain profitability.

7.5) Tokenized Yield Trading Within Delta-Neutral Strategies

Tokenized yield trading plays a crucial role in optimizing delta-neutral strategies by improving liquidity management and stabilizing returns. Effective management of counterparty concentration risk and return volatility is especially important for delta-neutral strategies to maintain stability and resilience. When integrated strategically, they provide precise control over yield exposure and risk distribution, strengthening the overall efficiency of delta-neutral portfolios.

Significance of Liquidity Management

One of the primary risks in delta-neutral strategies is counterparty exposure. A well-balanced strategy requires diversifying exposure across multiple platforms to reduce systemic risk. YT leverage enables participants to enhance yield exposure while maintaining balanced concentration risk thresholds. Efficient capital deployment without excessive exposure to a single counterparty is critical for delta-neutral strategies.

Significance of Fixed Yields

Beyond helping to reduce volatility in directional portfolios, PTs are particularly valuable in delta-neutral strategies, where they act as an effective hedge against unpredictable yield fluctuations.

Many delta-neutral strategies heavily rely on funding rate arbitrage, yet funding rates remain highly volatile and unpredictable. While direct ways to hedge perpetual funding rate movements do not currently exist, alternatives are emerging, such as Pendle Borros.

Until then, participants can use yield trading as an indirect hedge. Locking in a high fixed rate on assets such as sUSDe, which generate their yields from a basis trade, can serve as a counterbalance in case funding rates decline, improving the overall return profile of the strategy.

Managing Tail Risks

Many yield-bearing assets are stablecoin-based (e.g., sUSDe), requiring no further hedging to avoid a positive delta. Participants can also decide to hedge against insolvency risk by borrowing (then selling) the asset on a money market. *Note that this can only be done with rebasing assets, since borrowing interest-bearing assets will accrue yield on the debt, mostly canceling out returns.*

Assets tied to volatile base assets can be effectively hedged using money markets or derivatives:

- A participant holding PT-stETH can hedge exposure by shorting ETH on perpetual contracts and receive funding payments if funding rates are positive (which they are most of the time).

- Alternatively, borrowing and selling stETH is another way to hedge where the participant will not receive funding payment but is protected against protocol-specific risk, such as a Lido exploit. Once again, it can be done with stETH because it is a rebasing asset, but it cannot be done with wstETH because it is an interest-bearing asset.

Takeaways

Tokenized yield trading is essentially on-chain interest rate derivatives that offer a sophisticated toolset for refining delta-neutral strategies. Utilizing these instruments allows participants to optimize liquidity exposure, stabilize returns, and maintain a well-balanced yield structure. Used correctly, they provide greater resilience against counterparty risks and yield fluctuations while preserving the integrity of a delta-neutral approach.

Chapter 5: Current Tailwinds and Challenges

The landscape of delta-neutral strategies in DeFi is evolving rapidly, shaped by both favorable trends and structural challenges. On the one hand, emerging innovations in on-chain derivatives and AI are expanding market inefficiencies, creating new opportunities for agile participants. On the other hand, DeFi participants must navigate persistent risks, such as self-custody security concerns and regulatory uncertainty, which continue to influence market dynamics.

This chapter explores the key tailwinds and obstacles of delta-neutral strategies today. The first section examines how the growth of on-chain derivatives and AI-driven automation is transforming market structure and generating exploitable inefficiencies. The second section highlights the fundamental risks that remain, focusing on the challenges of self-custody and the uncertain regulatory landscape.

1. Current Tailwinds

Delta-neutral strategies in DeFi are currently benefiting from a rare convergence of favorable conditions. Structural inefficiencies persist, creating exploitable opportunities, while broader industry trends provide strong tailwinds for future growth. At the time of writing, two significant trends stand out: the continued expansion of on-chain derivatives and the increasing integration of AI into DeFi. The rise of on-chain derivatives is fragmenting liquidity and reducing reliance on CEXs, leading to new inefficiencies that can be systematically exploited. Meanwhile, AI-driven automation and data processing promise to refine market participation and unlock novel opportunities. These trends suggest that, while individual market conditions may shift, the underlying structural advantages for delta-neutral strategies will likely persist.

1.1) On-Chain Derivatives Growth

The expansion of on-chain derivatives is one of the most significant factors driving new opportunities for delta-neutral strategies. As the number of trading venues and derivative instruments increases, so do inefficiencies that traders can systematically exploit. A constantly expanding and innovating market is fertile ground for continuous opportunity. Individual participants, often more agile than institutional players, can gain a first-mover advantage in capturing new inefficiencies and generating profit before larger entities can adapt.

Hyperliquid Listings

Hyperliquid has rapidly gained market share in the DEX space, positioning itself as a dominant player. One of the many tailwinds for Hyperliquid is being very in touch with new assets and often being the first major exchange to list them. With many large players yet to transition on-chain, these listings frequently deviate significantly from index prices, creating extraordinary arbitrage opportunities—such as capturing a 30% price discrepancy between spot and perps prices within minutes.

The growing number of trading venues amplifies market inefficiencies during volatile events, such as token listings, presenting continuous opportunities for agile participants to capitalize on emerging discrepancies.

Hyperliquid Funding Rates

Hyperliquid's funding rates are structurally higher than those of CEXs, largely due to logistic challenges preventing larger players from transitioning on-chain. This sustained funding premium offers persistent yield advantages for those deploying delta-neutral strategies.

This type of structural inefficiency provides a consistent source of yield for participants who can identify and swiftly act on emerging opportunities.

Instrument Innovation

Beyond arbitrage, ongoing innovation in decentralized derivative instruments continues to broaden the spectrum of available strategies. For instance, the rise of permissionless options markets for altcoins enables traders to hedge LP positions in a new way, as their return profiles closely resemble each other. With more instruments available, market participants can construct more sophisticated structured strategies tailored to DeFi's evolving landscape.

The continued expansion of on-chain derivatives offers new tools and enables participants to execute structured, risk-managed strategies more flexibly in the evolving DeFi ecosystem.

1.2) Decentralized Finance and AI Synergy

The integration of AI into DeFi is still in its infancy. At the time of writing, the total market capitalization of the AI-DeFi sector is approximately $10 billion, with most projects in the early stages of development. Leaders are emerging, but the sector still lacks clear winners. However, the potential synergy between AI and DeFi is undeniable.

Despite DeFi's rapid evolution, it remains hindered by complexity and inefficiency, limiting broader adoption. AI-driven solutions aim to address these pain points, offering automation, optimization, and accessibility improvements. As the industry matures, the intersection of AI and DeFi—termed DeFAI—has the potential to revolutionize user experience and capital efficiency.

How AI Addresses Decentralized Finance's Challenges

i. **Reducing Complexity and Information Overload:** DeFi's expansive ecosystem includes over 1,500 DEXs, hundreds of yield-generating protocols, and millions of tradable assets. Information is scattered across multiple sources, such as Twitter, Telegram, Discord, and on-chain data, making it increasingly difficult for users—especially retail participants—to keep up.

AI-powered aggregation tools and sentiment analysis engines streamline information processing, allowing traders and investors to make informed decisions with less manual effort. These tools help users filter out noise, track relevant market movements, and identify profitable opportunities more efficiently.

ii. **Optimizing Capital Allocation:** Identifying optimal opportunities in DeFi requires sifting through vast amounts of fragmented data, and even after pinpointing profitable strategies, execution remains inefficient. Many strategies, such as concentrated liquidity provision and yield farming, demand continuous monitoring and adjustments. While automated liquidity management protocols and account abstraction solutions help reduce friction, they fall short of fully eliminating inefficiencies.

AI-powered tools can optimize these processes by:

- Identifying the most capital-efficient yield strategies in real time.

- Automatically rebalancing liquidity positions based on market conditions.

- Managing loan repayments and collateral adjustments to mitigate liquidation risks.

DeFAI could eliminate or at least reduce the need for constant manual oversight, allowing users to execute complex strategies with ease and efficiency.

AI-Powered Information Processing

Projects of this type focus on aggregating and analyzing on-chain and off-chain data to identify trends, risks, and opportunities. Users can query AI-driven agents for insights into token fundamentals, technical indicators, and sentiment analysis. The current leader in this category, AIXBT, features its own custom large language model (LLM), data indexer, and trend identification algorithm. Its market calls and trend predictions have established it as an important source within the DeFi community.

The integration of AI in real-time news processing has significantly improved accessibility, especially for retail users. Ambush, for instance, specializes in news interpretation and rapid on-chain event monitoring, delivering instant market-moving insights through AI-filtered alerts and natural language processing (NLP)-driven notifications. This allows traders to react swiftly to new information with one-click order execution. Unlike traditional financial tools such as Bloomberg, which can cost thousands of dollars per year, Ambush operates on an innovative business model that provides free access to users who execute trades via its referral links.

Improved UX Through Natural Language Processing

As DeFi products grow in complexity, AI-powered user interfaces simplify interactions through text-to-action functionalities. These interfaces allow users to execute sophisticated transactions using simple commands, streamlining multi-step and multi-chain processes.

Griffain is currently a market leader in AI-driven user experience improvements. It provides a suite of specialized agents tailored to various DeFi needs, including token sniping, automated execution, and strategy optimization.

NLP support is one of the fundamental innovations of AI; it is often implemented even in projects that do not focus on this functionality specifically. As mentioned above, Ambush supports NLP-driven notifications, for instance.

True Chain Abstraction: Eliminating Bridging and Fragmentation

One of DeFi's fundamental issues is blockchain fragmentation. Existing cross-chain solutions, such as bridges, introduce complexity, delays, and security risks. AI-driven chain abstraction is an idea that aims to eliminate these barriers entirely, creating a seamless, unified DeFi experience.

Key Innovations:

- **Elimination of Traditional Bridging:** Bridges only connect chains—they do not unify them. This isolates liquidity across networks, creating inefficiencies. AI-powered solutions aim to overcome this by enabling seamless interactions across ecosystems.

- **Unified Balance Across Chains:** AI-enabled chain abstraction allows users to maintain a singular chain-abstracted balance, removing the need to manually bridge assets between chains.

- **Instant Cross-Chain Transactions:** Instead of waiting for bridging delays, users can transact in real time, utilizing their entire balance across multiple chains instantly.

How It Works:

i. A DeFAI agent receives a user's transaction request and orchestrates the execution.

ii. A liquidity provider agent front-runs the transaction, supplying the required funds on the destination chain instantly.

iii. The liquidity provider agent settles the transaction by claiming funds from the user's wallet on other chains.

For example, if a user wants to mint an NFT on Solana using assets on Ethereum, the DeFAI agent coordinates with a liquidity provider agent to execute the transaction instantly. The user's cross-chain assets are settled in the background without manual intervention.

Takeaways

While the integration of AI into DeFi is still in its early stages, its long-term implications are profound. AI-driven automation, NLP-enhanced interfaces, and chain abstraction solutions have the potential to redefine how users interact with DeFi protocols.

As AI adoption grows, it will introduce new inefficiencies and opportunities, fueling the next wave of financial innovation. Traders and LPs who stay ahead of these advancements will be well-positioned to capitalize on the evolving DeFi landscape.

2. **Current Challenges**

DeFi offers significant opportunities, but it also comes with inherent risks that all participants must navigate. Unlike traditional finance, where centralized entities provide security, regulatory compliance, and financial protections, DeFi operates on a permissionless and trust-minimized framework. This shift creates new challenges that impact all market participants, even those employing delta-neutral strategies.

The risks within DeFi are structural rather than market-based; they persist regardless of an investor's strategy or risk appetite. While delta-neutral strategies mitigate exposure to price volatility, they do not eliminate risks tied to self-custody, smart contract vulnerabilities, counterparty risks, and regulatory uncertainty.

This section examines two major challenges inherent to DeFi. First, self-custody, which places full responsibility on users for securing their assets, presents both an advantage and a burden. While it removes reliance on intermediaries, it demands strong operational security (OPSEC) to prevent theft and loss. Second, the unclear and evolving regulatory landscape creates an uncertain environment for DeFi protocols and their users, as global regulatory approaches vary widely.

Navigating these challenges requires careful planning, risk management, and an awareness of both security best practices and regulatory trends. The following subsections will provide deeper insights into these risks and discuss methods for mitigating their impact.

2.1) Responsibility of Self-Custody

Self-custody is one of the defining features of DeFi. Unlike CeFi, where intermediaries hold and manage assets on behalf of users, DeFi requires participants to take full control of their funds. This removes reliance on third parties but introduces the personal responsibility of securing assets against theft, hacks, and accidental loss.

The ability to transact without permission and maintain full ownership of assets is a powerful advantage, but it comes with significant risks. Security failures in DeFi are often irreversible. Without a centralized authority to recover stolen or lost funds, users must implement strong OPSEC measures to protect themselves.

Cold Wallets and Private Key Security

Using a hardware wallet (cold wallet) like Ledger or Trezor is one of the most effective ways to secure digital assets. These devices store private keys offline, making them highly resistant to online attacks. However, they should always be purchased directly from the manufacturer or an authorized seller to avoid tampering risks.

While cold wallets protect private keys from online threats, they do not defend against all attack vectors. It is important to remain vigilant against other security risks that could compromise funds.

Awareness of Attack Vectors

DeFi participants face a variety of attack methods, including:

- Phishing scams that trick users into revealing private keys.

- Approval scams where deceptive contracts trick users into granting full access to their funds.

- Address poisoning, where attackers create addresses similar to those frequently used by a target to mislead them into sending funds to the wrong address.

- Honeypots and rug pulls, where malicious actors create projects that appear legitimate but are designed to steal funds.

While it is very difficult to grasp all attack vectors and their nuances, recognizing the most common ones is a powerful safeguard against potential threats.

Smart Contract Risk and Diversification

Risk-zero does not exist in DeFi (or anywhere else), even well-audited smart contracts are not immune to exploits. Unexpected vulnerabilities can be discovered, leading to significant financial losses. Just as diversification is crucial for portfolios with directional risk, it is equally essential for DeFi strategies. Spreading exposure across multiple protocols, wallets, and blockchains minimizes the impact of potential failures or security breaches.

Takeaways

Self-custody grants users sovereignty over their assets but demands vigilance. Practicing strong OPSEC is essential for protecting against the risks inherent to DeFi. While self-custody eliminates reliance on third parties, it also means that security is entirely the user's responsibility.

2.2) Honorable Mention: Unclear Regulatory Landscape

DeFi operates in a largely unregulated and inconsistent legal environment. As DeFi continues to grow, regulators worldwide are paying closer attention, raising concerns about compliance, security, and financial stability. However, the absence of clear, unified regulatory frameworks leaves protocols and users uncertain about the future.

Jurisdictional Differences

DeFi's global nature means it faces varying regulatory approaches depending on the jurisdiction. Some countries are embracing DeFi and blockchain innovation, while others impose strict restrictions or outright bans. This fragmentation creates challenges for projects operating across multiple regions, forcing them to adapt to different legal landscapes or relocate to more favorable environments.

Impact on Users and Protocols

Uncertainty in regulations poses risks for both DeFi protocols and their users:

- Protocols may face legal action, fines, or shutdowns due to non-compliance with evolving regulations.

- Users risk losing access to platforms if regulatory crackdowns force services to cease operations or restrict participation.

- Increased compliance requirements, such as KYC and AML measures, could undermine DeFi's permissionless nature and reduce accessibility for global users.

Current Regulatory Trends

- **Europe:** The Markets in Crypto-Assets (MiCA) framework is an attempt to unify crypto regulation across the European Union. While it primarily focuses on centralized crypto services, its impact on DeFi remains uncertain. If stricter measures are introduced, DeFi projects may be required to adopt compliance mechanisms similar to centralized platforms.

- **United States:** Regulatory clarity in the US remains limited. Agencies such as the SEC and CFTC continue to debate how DeFi falls within existing financial regulations. However, recent political shifts, including a more crypto-friendly administration, indicate potential progress toward clearer guidelines.

- **Asia:** Japan has historically maintained strict regulations but has recently adopted a more accommodating stance toward crypto businesses. Meanwhile, Hong Kong, once a hub for crypto activity, has seen a decline due to regulatory uncertainty and its alignment with China's restrictive policies. Singapore has been following a more balanced approach.

Takeaways

DeFi's long-term success depends, in part, on how regulatory frameworks evolve. While regulatory uncertainty poses risks, DeFi continues to innovate and adapt to emerging compliance requirements. Staying informed about legal developments is essential for both projects and users as the landscape continues to shift.

Glossary

Arbitrage – A trading strategy that exploits discrepancies across different markets to generate risk-free or low-risk profits.

AMM: Automated Market Maker – A decentralized exchange mechanism that enables users to trade assets through liquidity pools instead of traditional order books.

Backwardation – A market condition where futures trade below the spot price.

Basis Trade – A strategy that captures the difference between the spot price of an asset and its futures price, often used in delta-neutral strategies.

Beta-Adjusted Delta – Delta accounting for differences in volatility and correlation between assets.

Bid-Ask Spread – The difference between the highest price a buyer is willing to pay for an asset and the lowest price a seller is willing to accept, often used in the context of order books.

Capital Efficiency – A measure of how effectively capital is utilized in a strategy, optimizing risk-adjusted returns while minimizing unused liquidity.

Cash-and-Carry Arbitrage – A strategy that exploits the price difference between an asset's spot price and its futures price by buying in the spot market and shorting the futures contract to capture a risk-free return.

CeFi: Centralized Finance – Traditional financial infrastructure where transactions and financial services are facilitated by centralized entities like banks or exchanges.

Collateralized Loan – A loan backed by assets that the borrower pledges as security, allowing lenders to seize the collateral in the event of default.

Composability – The ability of decentralized finance (DeFi) protocols to interact seamlessly with one another, allowing users to build and execute complex financial strategies.

Contango – A market condition where futures trade above the spot price.

Counterparty Risk – The risk that the other party in a financial transaction, such as an exchange or lending platform, may default on its obligations.

CPV: Counterparty Vault – A smart contract-based liquidity pool where users deposit assets to provide liquidity, typically to a decentralized perpetual exchange. The CPV serves as the counterparty to traders, earning fees and net PNL.

DEX: Decentralized Exchange – A peer-to-peer marketplace where cryptocurrency transactions occur directly between users without intermediaries.

DeFi: Decentralized Finance – A financial ecosystem built on blockchain technology that allows for open, permissionless access to financial services such as lending, borrowing, and trading.

DeFAI: Decentralized Finance and AI Synergy – The intersection of DeFi and AI-driven solutions, where automation, optimization, and enhanced data processing improve market participation and efficiency.

Delta – A measure of how much the price of a derivative or hedging instrument changes in response to movements in the underlying asset.

Delta-Neutral Strategy – A trading strategy that seeks to minimize directional market exposure by balancing long and short positions, allowing traders to profit from market inefficiencies rather than price movements.

Drawdown – A peak-to-trough decline in portfolio value, often expressed as a percentage.

EMH: Efficient Market Hypothesis – A theory stating that asset prices reflect all available information, making it impossible to consistently achieve excess returns without taking additional risk.

Equity Market – A marketplace where company shares are issued and traded.

Exchange Rate Oracle – An oracle pricing method that bases values on fundamental backing rather than market fluctuations.

EV: Expected Value – A probability-weighted measure of potential returns, used to assess the long-term profitability of a trading strategy.

Fixed-Income Instrument – A type of investment that provides regular, predictable interest payments.

Flash Loans – Uncollateralized DeFi loans that must be repaid within a single transaction.

Forex Market: Foreign Exchange Market – A global, decentralized market for trading national currencies.

Funding Rate – A periodic payment between long and short traders in perpetual futures markets.

Health Factor – A risk metric used in DeFi lending markets to assess the safety of a borrower's position.

Hedging – A risk management technique that involves taking offsetting positions to reduce exposure to price movements.

Impermanent Loss – A structural inefficiency in AMMs where liquidity providers (LPs) lose value as asset prices diverge, allowing arbitrageurs to extract profits. IL occurs due to AMMs' rigid pricing, making LPs systematically disadvantaged unless offset by fees.

Intermarket Correlation – The relationship between different asset classes or markets.

Intrinsic Lending Yield – The natural return generated from lending assets in DeFi platforms.

Leverage – The use of borrowed funds to amplify potential returns.

Limit Order – A type of order to buy or sell an asset at a specified price.

Liquidity – The degree to which an asset can be bought or sold in the market.

Liquidity Fragmentation – The dispersion of trading activity across multiple exchanges, often causing inefficiencies.

Liquidity Mining – A mechanism where users provide liquidity to DeFi protocols in exchange for rewards.

Liquidity Premium – The additional return demanded by investors for holding less liquid assets.

LP: Liquidity Provider – A participant who supplies assets to a liquidity pool to facilitate trading and earn fees.

LRT: Liquid Restaked Token – A token representing staked assets that have been restaked for additional security incentives.

Looping – The recursive process of borrowing, selling, and supplying the same asset in lending markets to amplify exposure, effectively creating leverage.

LSD: Liquid Staking Derivative – A token representing staked assets that remains liquid and usable in DeFi.

Margin Requirement – The minimum amount of collateral required to maintain a leveraged position.

Market Efficiency – The extent to which asset prices reflect all available information.

Market Inefficiency – A condition in which an asset's price deviates from its fair value.

Market Making –A trading activity that involves providing liquidity to markets by continuously quoting buy and sell prices for an asset.

Market Microstructure – The study of how different trading mechanisms, order flows, and transaction costs impact price formation and market liquidity.

Money Market – A sector of financial markets dealing with short-term borrowing and lending.

Open Interest – The total number of outstanding derivative contracts, such as futures or options, that have not been settled.

OPSEC: Operational Security – Practices to protect sensitive information and assets from security threats.

OTC: Over-the-Counter Market – A market where financial instruments are traded directly between parties without a centralized exchange.

Perpetual Futures – A type of futures contract without an expiration date.

Points-Based Incentives – A rewards mechanism where protocols issue non-tokenized incentives (e.g., points) to encourage liquidity provision, trading, or borrowing activities.

Price Discovery – The process by which markets determine the fair price of an asset based on supply and demand dynamics.

PT: Principal Token – A financial instrument that represents the principal component of a yield-bearing asset.

Restaking – Extending the utility of staked assets by securing additional protocols.

Risk-Adjusted Return – A measure of profitability that accounts for the level of risk taken to generate returns. Delta-neutral strategies aim to optimize risk-adjusted returns by minimizing volatility while capturing inefficiencies.

Risk Aversion – Investors' preference for lower-risk assets, even at the cost of lower expected returns. Risk-averse investors prioritize capital preservation and favor investments with more predictable outcomes over those with higher volatility and potential losses.

Risk-Free Rate – The theoretical return on an investment with no risk of financial loss, often used as a benchmark for evaluating other investments.

Risk Management – The process of identifying, assessing, and mitigating risks in a trading strategy.

Risk of Self-Custody – The responsibility of individuals to securely manage their private keys and assets in DeFi, eliminating reliance on intermediaries but increasing exposure to security risks.

Slippage – The difference between the expected price of a trade and the actual executed price, often due to market volatility or low liquidity.

Smart Contract – A self-executing contract with the terms directly written into code, allowing for automated financial transactions without intermediaries.

Spot Market – A market where assets are bought and sold for immediate settlement and delivery at the prevailing price.

Systemic Risk – The risk of widespread financial instability caused by the interconnectedness of institutions and markets.

Tail Risk – The risk of rare and extreme events that cause significant market disruption and are not captured by standard risk models.

Tokenized Yield-Trading – Yield-bearing assets separated into tradable tokens, allowing participants to speculate on or hedge future yield movements.

TVL: Total Value Locked – The total capital deposited in a DeFi protocol.

Variance – The degree to which returns fluctuate over time.

Volatility – A statistical measure of an asset's price fluctuations over time, affecting the risk and profitability of trading strategies.

Yield Curve Inefficiencies – Discrepancies in the expected returns of assets over different durations.

YT: Yield Token – A tokenized asset that represents the yield portion of a yield-bearing asset, allowing traders to speculate on or hedge future yield fluctuations.

www.ingramcontent.com/pod-product-compliance
Lightning Source LLC
Chambersburg PA
CBHW021922190326
41519CB00009B/881